The Rag Doll Book

THE RAG DOLL BOOK

15 DELIGHTFUL DOLLS TO MAKE

PETRA BOASE

EBURY PRESS
LONDON

First published in 1995 by Ebury Press Limited
1 3 5 7 9 10 8 6 4 2

Edited by **Emma Callery**
Designed by **Alison Shackleton**
Photography by **Shona Wood**
Illustrations by **Tony Hannaford**

Ebury Press Limited
Random House, 20 Vauxhall Bridge Road,
London SW1V 2SA

Random House Australia (Pty) Limited
20 Alfred Street, Milsons Point, Sydney,
New South Wales 2061, Australia

Random House New Zealand Limited
18 Poland Road, Glenfield, Auckland 10, New Zealand

Random House South Africa (Pty) Limited
PO Box 337, Bergvlei, South Africa

Random House UK Limited Reg. No 954009

A CIP catalogue record for this book is available from the British Library

ISBN 0 09 180819 7

Printed in Italy by New Interlitho

CONTENTS

INTRODUCTION

Rag dolls have wonderful personalities of their own, which are created by you the maker. One of the most enjoyable parts of making the dolls is spending time collecting together the fabrics and trimmings. Always look in the remnants box in haberdashery stores to see if there are any small fabric pieces that might be suitable. Jumble and car boot sales are also good haunts for finding interesting fabrics.

This book has been devised so that rag doll making is as straightforward and as fun as possible. I have begun by showing you how to make the dolls' bodies (see opposite) which, after all, is the basic requirement for any rag doll. I then move onto the dolls themselves which are divided into two groups - some traditional dolls from around the world and then some fantasy dolls all ready for a fancy dress party. Finally, there are the pattern pieces and a list of suppliers.

I must emphasize here that dressing dolls is a personal matter and while I show you exactly how to reproduce the dolls featured in the photographs, I think it is important that you should feel free to experiment in whatever way you like. In this way you make your doll unique. Hair styles, facial expressions, clothing, can all be changed - go ahead, experiment. I have really enjoyed making these dolls, and I hope you will too and end up feeling as attached to them as I now do.

THE PATTERN PIECES

The pattern pieces given in this book are life size, so they can be traced or photocopied. There is no fiddly enlarging to contend with. The patterns are also a useful guideline to let you know how much fabric you need for each piece of clothing. Each pattern has been marked with a seam allowance, too, so there is no need to worry about adding that to the pattern pieces. Where a pattern crosses the page you will need to fill in the gap between the two halves of the pattern. Use a pencil and ruler to make a good straight line.

WARNING: These rag dolls are not suitable for children under the age of three as they have detachable parts.

OPPOSITE: The plump doll (left) and the thin doll (right) are both made in exactly the same way; it's just their dimensions that vary.

MAKING THE BODIES

The following instructions apply to all three body patterns - plump, thin and baby - featured on pages 44-52. The materials needed for the relevant body are listed at the top of each doll's materials list.

THE PATTERNS

PLUMP DOLL'S BODY: see pages 44-7
THIN DOLL'S BODY: see pages 48-50
BABY DOLL'S BODY: see pages 51-2

CUTTING OUT

BODY, ARMS AND LEGS: cut from calico or cotton fabrics
HEAD: cut from cotton jersey

1 With right sides facing, machine stitch one of the head pieces to one of the body pieces with a 5mm (¼in) seam. Repeat for the other pieces. Press the seams open.

2 With right sides facing, sew the body and head pieces together with a 5mm (¼in) seam. Leave a sufficient gap at the bottom of the body for the stuffing . Turn the body right sides out.

3 Fill the body with stuffing until it is firm and sew up the gap. You may need to use a knitting needle to ensure the stuffing goes right to the furthest corners.

4 With right sides facing, machine stitch the arms and the legs, again leaving an opening at the top of each limb for the stuffing to go in. Press the seams open and turn the pieces right sides out.

5 Fill each piece to the top with stuffing.

6 Pinch in the top of each limb and hand stitch the opening to close it.

7 Following the markings on each body pattern, firmly stitch the limbs in place.

◆HINTS AND TIPS◆

◆ If you are tracing the pattern pieces at the back of the book, mark and label them as in the book.

◆ Always pin the pattern pieces on the straight of grain. This is particularly important if you are cutting out stripy or checked material as your doll will undoubtedly prefer to wear clothes that don't look crooked.

◆ If you need to fold fabric when cutting it out, always do so with the right sides facing and on the straight of grain.

◆ Before stitching anything it is best to at least pin fabrics together, and preferably baste them too, for a neater end result.

◆ Attention to detail when making up the costumes is very important. The simplest hand stitching or trimming can complete and make a doll's outfit. So never feel restrained when it comes to those finishing touches.

TRADITIONAL DOLLS

In this chapter there is a selection of rag dolls dressed from around the world. Each is wearing very suitable clothing, ranging from the practical Shaker Boy and Girl, to the warmly-clad Inuit and those Party Girls, dressed in their brightest, most cheerful partywear. What a colourful group they make.

FLOWER GIRL

In order to create this sweet and delicate doll it is important to spend time looking for the appropriate fabrics that will work well together. Sew small ribbon rosebuds on parts of the dress and style her hair with paper or fabric flowers.

YOU WILL NEED

FOR THE BODY
- 46 x 46cm (18 x 18in) calico or cotton
- 18 x 36cm (7 x 14in) cotton jersey
- Scissors
- Dressmaker's pins
- Cotton threads (to match fabrics)
- Sewing machine
- Iron and ironing board
- Needle
- 250g (8oz) washable stuffing

FOR THE CLOTHES
- Fabrics (see patterns for quantity)
- Pinking shears
- 61cm (24in) piece 5mm (¼in) wide elastic
- Safety pin
- 30cm (12in) strip fasteners or velcro
- 3 x 15mm (⅝in) self-cover buttons
- Assortment of ribbon roses (sizes and colours)

FOR THE HAIR AND FACE
- 1 ball wool (yellow)
- 10cm (4in) bias binding (yellow)
- Fabric glue
- Paper or fabric flowers
- 11mm (⅜in) self-cover button
- Tailor's chalk
- Embroidery threads (red, yellow)
- Scrap felt (black)

CUTTING OUT

BODY: thin doll's pattern pieces, pages 48-50
SHOES: thin doll's pattern piece, page 53
CLOTHES: pattern pieces, pages 54-7

◆ BODY ◆

Make up the body as on page 7.

◆ SHOES ◆

1 Fold the top edge of each shoe over by 5mm (¼in), carefully press and then machine stitch in place.
2 Machine stitch each shoe together with right sides facing. Press the seams open and turn right sides out.

◆ PANTALOONS ◆

1 Keep each piece of the pantaloons folded with the right sides facing and machine stitch along the inside leg with a 5mm (¼in) seam. Press the seams open.
2 Turn one leg piece right side out and place it inside the other, matching up the raw edges of the centre (crotch) seam. Machine stitch the two pieces together, again using a 5mm (¼in) seam. Press the seam flat and turn the pantaloons completely inside out.
3 At the bottom, turn up 3cm (1¼in) on the inside. Machine stitch a line 15mm (⅝in) from the fold leaving a 12mm (½in) gap through which to insert the elastic. Then stitch another line 5mm (¼in) from the bottom fold. Trim the raw edges with pinking shears. Insert a length of elastic into each casing using a safety pin to guide it. Gather, stitch the ends of the elastic together and cut off the excess.
4 At the waist, turn over 3cm (1¼in) to the wrong side and machine stitch all around 1cm (⅜in) from the fold. Leave a 12mm (½in) gap through which to insert the elastic. Trim the raw edges with pinking shears and insert and finish off the elastic as for the legs.

◆ DRESS ◆

1 Machine stitch the dress front to the back pieces at the shoulders with a 5mm (¼in) seam. Press the seams flat.
2 Place the sleeves on the shoulders with the centre of the sleeve matching the centre seam of the shoulder and with the right sides facing. Baste together and then machine stitch. Allow a 5mm (¼in) seam; press open when finished.
3 On each cuff of the sleeves and the hem, turn over 1cm (⅜in) of fabric and press. Machine stitch floral bias binding on to it.
4 With right sides facing and starting at the end of each sleeve, sew up the side seam of the first sleeve and down the side of the dress allowing a 5mm (¼in) seam. Repeat on the other side. Press the seams open.

5 Press the neck seam over to neaten and machine stitch floral bias binding onto it .
6 On each side at the back opening, turn over 2cm (¾in) to the wrong side and machine stitch. Trim the raw edges with pinking shears.
7 To hold the dress closed, sew on a line of fasteners or a strip of velcro. Cover the 15mm (⅝in) buttons with fabric and sew a small ribbon rose onto each one. Attach the buttons to the centre front of the dress in a line.
8 Decorate the dress with small ribbon roses.

◆ HAIR ◆

1 Cut approximately 100 strands of wool for the main hair (this is only a guideline as it is up to you how thick and long you wish to make the hair). Lay the centre of the strands of wool evenly on a strip of similar-coloured bias binding and sew them down. If you have problems keeping the wool still while sewing, fasten them down with a dab of fabric glue.
2 For the fringe, cut approximately 50 strands to the same length as the main hair. Lay on another strip of bias binding, 5cm (2in) in from one end of the strands. Secure as before.
3 To attach the hair to the doll's head, first sew down the fringe piece, with the strip of binding running over the head from side to side. Do this using a similar coloured thread and small running stitches. Then attach the main hair piece so that it runs at right angles to the other piece, forming a parting in the middle. Trim the hair to the desired length.
4 Sew paper or fabric flowers into the hair.

◆ FACE ◆

1 Cover the 11mm (⅜in) button with a piece of the face fabric and stitch onto the face, slightly below the centre. Mark the shape of the mouth with a piece of tailor's chalk. Using red embroidery thread, stitch on the mouth.
2 For the eyes, cut two small circles out of the black felt and stick them on to the face. Sew eyelashes with yellow lines of embroidery.

SHAKER BOY

Following in the style of the American Shakers, simplicity and function are the key elements in the clothing of this doll. For his trousers I've used a denim fabric for style and strength, and for the shirt I've used a plain check - the ultimate functional costume for a day on the farm with his faithful cows. The gingham ribbon scarf will keep his neck warm whatever the weather and it smartly coordinates with all his other checked clothing.

YOU WILL NEED

FOR THE BODY

- 46 x 46cm (18 x 18in) calico or cotton
- 18 x 36cm (7 x 14in) cotton jersey
- Scissors
- Dressmaker's pins
- Cotton threads (to match fabrics)
- Sewing machine
- Iron and ironing board
- Needle
- 250g (8oz) washable stuffing

FOR THE CLOTHES

- Fabrics (see patterns for quantity)
- Pinking shears
- 50cm (20in) piece 5mm (¼in) wide elastic
- Safety pin
- Heart button
- 18cm (7in) strip fasteners or velcro
- 25cm (12in) gingham ribbon

FOR THE HAIR AND FACE

- 1 ball wool (brown)
- 11mm (⅜in) self-cover button
- Tailor's chalk
- Embroidery thread (red)
- Scrap felt (black)
- Fabric glue

CUTTING OUT

BODY: thin doll's pattern pieces, pages 48-50
CLOTHES AND SHOES: pattern pieces, pages 58-61

◆ BODY ◆

Make up the body using the thin doll pattern on pages 48-50 and following the instructions on page 7.

◆ SHOES ◆

1 Carefully cut out four pieces of fabric from the pattern.
2 Fold the top edge of each shoe over by 5mm (¼in) and machine stitch down.
3 Machine stitch each shoe together with right sides facing. Press the seams open and turn right sides out.

◆ TROUSERS ◆

1 Keep each piece of the trousers folded with the right sides facing and machine stitch along the inside leg with a 5mm (¼in) seam. Press the seams open.
2 Turn one leg piece right side out and place it inside the other, matching up the raw edges of the centre (crotch) seam. Machine stitch the two pieces together, again using a 5mm (¼in) seam. Press the seam flat and turn the inside leg out so that the garment is the wrong side out completely.
3 At the bottom of the legs, turn up 1cm (⅜in) of fabric to make a hem and machine stitch along this hem line.
4 At the waist, turn over 3cm (1¼in) to the wrong side and machine stitch all around, 1cm (⅜in) from the fold and leaving a 12mm (½in) gap through which to insert the elastic. Trim the raw edges with pinking shears.
5 Insert a length of elastic into the casing using a safety pin to guide it. Gather to an appropriate size and stitch the ends of the elastic together cutting off the excess.

◆ SHIRT ◆

1 Machine stitch the shirt front to the back pieces at the shoulders with a 5mm (¼in) seam. Press the seams flat.
2 Place the sleeves on the shoulders with the centre of the sleeve matching the centre seam of the shoulder and with the right sides facing. You might find it easier to baste the pieces together before machine stitching. Allow a 5mm (¼in) seam and press the seams open when finished.
3 On each cuff of the sleeve, turn over 1cm (⅜in) of fabric to the wrong side, press thoroughly and machine stitch. Do the same at the hem.
4 With right sides facing and starting at the end of each sleeve, sew up the side seam of the first sleeve and down the side of the shirt allowing a 5mm (¼in) seam. Repeat on the other side. Press the seams open.
5 For the motif, fray the edges of the square by pulling out some of the threads. Then attach the heart to the square with a contrasting coloured running stitch and sew a small heart button onto the heart. Hand stitch the motif onto the front of the shirt, using a contrasting coloured running stitch.
6 Press the neck seam over to neaten and machine stitch.
7 On each side at the back opening, turn over 2cm (¾in) to the wrong side and machine stitch. Trim the raw edges with pinking shears.
8 To hold the shirt closed, sew on a line of fasteners or a strip of velcro.
9 Tie the gingham ribbon carefully around his neck with the knot at the front.

◆ HAIR ◆

1 Cut approximately 100 strands of wool all the same length and tie a piece of wool around the centre of them. Pull tight and knot firmly in place.
2 Hand sew the knot onto the top of the head and arrange the hair to create a style, trimming as necessary.

◆ FACE ◆

1 Cover the 11mm (⅜in) button with a piece of the face fabric and stitch onto the face, slightly below the centre.
2 Mark the shape of the mouth with a piece of tailor's chalk. Using red embroidery thread, stitch on the mouth.
3 For the eyes, cut two small circles out of the black felt and stick them onto the face.

SHAKER GIRL

The simple style of the American Shakers has a devoted following, for its plain style and clear colours. Here I have adapted the traditional look for a robust country doll. Dressed in a variety of homely cotton checks, she is ready for the duties on the farm.

YOU WILL NEED

FOR THE BODY

- 31 x 100cm (12 x 39in) calico or cotton
- 18 x 40cm (7 x 16in) cotton jersey
- Scissors
- Dressmaker's pins
- Cotton threads (to match fabrics)
- Sewing machine
- Iron and ironing board
- Needle
- 250g (8oz) washable stuffing

FOR THE CLOTHES

- Fabrics (see patterns for quantities)
- Pinking shears
- 81cm (32in) piece 5mm (¼in) wide elastic
- Safety pin
- 41cm (16in) elasticated checked ribbon
- Heart button
- 20cm (8in) rick-rack braid
- 30cm (12in) strip fasteners or velcro

FOR THE HAIR AND FACE

- 1 ball wool (black)
- 10cm (4in) bias binding (black)
- Fabric glue
- 20cm (8in) checked ribbon
- 11mm (⅜in) self-cover button
- Tailor's chalk
- Embroidery threads (red, black)
- Scraps felt (black, blue)

CUTTING OUT

BODY: plump doll's pattern pieces, pages 44-7
SHOES: plump doll's pattern piece, page 53
DRESS DECORATION: shirt motif pattern pieces, page 59
CLOTHES: pattern pieces, pages 62-5

◆ BODY ◆

Make up the body following the instructions on page 7.

◆ SHOES ◆

Make up the shoes following the instructions on page 10.

◆ PANTALOONS ◆

1 Keep each piece of the pantaloons folded with the right sides facing and machine stitch along the inside leg with a 5mm (¼in) seam. Press the seams open.

2 Turn one leg piece right side out and place it inside the other, matching up the raw edges of the centre (crotch) seam. Machine stitch the two pieces together, again using a 5mm (¼in) seam. Press the seam flat and turn the inside leg out so that the garment is the wrong side out completely.

3 At the bottom of the legs, turn up 3cm (1¼in) on the inside to make a hem. Machine stitch a line 15mm (⅝in) from the bottom fold of the hem leaving a 12mm (½in) gap through which to insert the elastic, and then machine stitch another line 5mm (¼in) from the bottom fold. Trim the raw edge with pinking shears. Insert a length of elastic into each casing using a safety pin to guide it. Gather to an appropriate size and stitch the ends of the elastic together cutting off the excess.

4 At the waist, turn over 3cm (1¼in) to the wrong side and machine stitch all around 1cm (⅜in) from the fold. Leave a 12mm (½in) gap through which to insert the elastic. Trim the raw edges with pinking shears and insert and finish off the elastic as for the legs.

◆ DRESS ◆

1 Machine stitch the dress front to the back pieces at the shoulders with a 5mm (¼in) seam. Press the seams flat.

2 Place the sleeves on the shoulders with the centre of the sleeve matching the centre seam of the shoulder and with the right sides facing. You might find it easier to baste the pieces together before machine stitching. Allow a 5mm (¼in) seam and press the seams open when finished.

3 On each cuff of the sleeve turn over 1cm (⅜in) of fabric to the wrong side and press. Machine stitch a strip of the elasticated checked ribbon along the cuffs.

4 For the hem, turn over 1cm (⅜in) and machine stitch in place.

5 With right sides facing and starting at the end of each sleeve, sew up the side seam of the first sleeve and down the side of the dress allowing a 5mm (¼in) seam. Repeat on the other side. Press the seams open.

6 For the motif, fray the edges of the square by pulling out some of the threads. Then attach the heart to the square with a running stitch in contrasting coloured thread, and sew a small heart button onto the heart. Hand stitch the motif onto the front of the dress, using contrasting coloured running stitch.

7 Press the neck seam over and machine stitch on a piece of rick-rack braid.

8 On each side at the back opening, turn over 2cm (⅜in) to the wrong side, press and machine stitch. Trim the raw edges with pinking shears.

9 To hold the dress closed, sew on a line of fasteners or a strip of velcro.

◆ HAIR ◆

1 Make up the hair following Steps 1 to 3 on page 10.

2 Divide the hair evenly into two bunches and plait them. Tie a checked bow at the end of each plait.

◆ FACE ◆

1 Cover the 11mm (⅜in) button with a piece of the face fabric and stitch onto the face, slightly below the centre.

2 Mark the shape of the mouth with a piece of tailor's chalk. Using red embroidery thread, stitch on the mouth.

3 Cut two small oval shapes out of the black felt and stick them onto the face. Cut two smaller circles out of the blue felt and stick them onto the black felt. Finally, sew small black lines of embroidery thread to make her lovely long eyelashes.

PARLOUR MAID

This is one of the more traditional dolls in the book. I had great fun searching around secondhand shops and car boot sales looking for old linen fabrics with interesting trimmings. I then cut them up to make this very pretty outfit.

YOU WILL NEED

FOR THE BODY

- 31 x 100cm (12 x 39in) calico or cotton
- 18 x 40cm (7 x 16in) cotton jersey
- Scissors
- Dressmaker's pins
- Cotton threads (to match fabrics)
- Sewing machine
- Iron and ironing board
- Needle
- 250g (8oz) washable stuffing

FOR THE CLOTHES

- Fabrics (see patterns for quantity)
- Pinking shears
- 1.5m (5ft) piece 5mm (¼in) wide elastic
- Safety pin
- 3m (10ft) assorted cotton lace trimmings and braids
- 30cm (12in) strip fasteners or velcro
- 20cm (8in) white cotton ribbon

FOR THE HAIR AND FACE

- 1 ball wool (brown)
- 10cm (4in) bias binding (brown)
- Fabric glue
- 11mm (⅜in) self-cover button
- Tailor's chalk
- Embroidery threads (red, yellow)
- Scrap felt (black)

CUTTING OUT

BODY: plump doll's pattern pieces, pages 44-47
SHOES: plump doll's pattern piece, page 53
CLOTHES: pattern pieces, pages 66-69; plus pantaloons on pages 62-63

◆ BODY ◆

Make up the body as on page 7.

◆ SHOES ◆

Make up the shoes as on page 10.

◆ PANTALOONS ◆

Make up the pantaloons as on page 10.

◆ PETTICOAT ◆

1 With the right sides facing, sew the two pieces of fabric together along the side seams allowing a 5mm (¼in) seam. Press open.
2 At the waist, turn over 3cm (1¼in) to the wrong side and machine stitch all around 1cm (⅜in) from the fold leaving a 12mm (½in) gap. Trim the raw edges with pinking shears. Insert the elastic as for the pantaloons, above.
3 At the hem, turn over 1cm (⅜in) to the wrong side and baste on a piece of lace braid. Machine stitch down.

◆ DRESS ◆

1 Machine stitch the dress front to the back pieces at the shoulders with a 5mm (¼in) seam. Press the seams flat.
2 Place the sleeves on the shoulders with the centre of the sleeve matching the centre seam of the shoulder and with the right sides facing. You might find it easier to baste the pieces together before machine stitching. Allow a 5mm (¼in) seam and press the seams open when finished.
3 With right sides facing and starting at the end of each sleeve, sew up the side seam of the first sleeve and down the side of the dress allowing a 5mm (¼in) seam. Repeat on the other side. Press the seams open.
4 On the wrong side and using zigzag stitch, machine stitch a length of the elastic around the waist of the dress.
5 Press the neck seam over to neaten and machine stitch a piece of narrow cotton lace on the inside of the neck, so that it stands up. Machine stitch another piece of cotton lace on the outside of the neck.
6 Turn the cuffs under making a 5mm (¼in) hem and over stitch a piece of cotton lace around the edge of the cuff. Repeat at the hem of the dress.
7 On each side at the back opening, turn over 2cm (¾in) to the wrong side and machine stitch. Trim the raw edges with pinking shears.

Onto one of the sides, machine stitch a strip of cotton lace.
8 To hold the dress closed, sew on a line of fasteners or a strip of velcro.

◆ APRON ◆

1 Machine stitch the two pieces of fabric together with right sides facing, leaving a small gap for turning.
2 Turn the apron right sides out, over stitch the opening to close and press. Sew a piece of cotton lace trimming onto the top edge of the apron to tie around the doll's waist.

◆ HAIR ◆

1 Cut approximately 100 strands of wool for the main hair (this is only a guideline as it is up to you how thick and long you wish to make the hair). Lay the centre of the strands of wool evenly on a strip of similar-coloured bias binding and sew them down using either hand or machine stitch. If you have problems keeping the wool strands still while sewing you can always fasten them down with a dab of fabric glue.
2 Sew the hair onto the head so that the parting lies in the centre. Use a similar-coloured thread and small running stitches.
3 Tie the hair at the back in a bunch and plait it. Fasten the end with a piece of wool.

◆ BONNET ◆

1 Machine stitch the two pieces of fabric together with right sides facing, leaving a small gap for turning.
2 Turn the bonnet right sides out, over stitch the opening to close and press. Sew a piece of cotton ribbon along the straight edge.
3 At each corner of the bonnet sew on a piece of ribbon, to tie beneath the doll's chin in a bow.

◆ FACE ◆

Make up the face as on page 10.

PARTY GIRLS - BIG SISTER

These jolly girls are dressed for some party fun. I've used an assortment of bright fabrics, coordinating them through the two outfits, so that the girls look good together. The hand-covered buttons make each outfit individual. On this page you will find instructions for making the Big Sister, and overleaf there are the instructions for making the Little Sister.

YOU WILL NEED

FOR THE BODY

- 64 x 46cm (25 x 18in) brown felt
- Scissors
- Dressmaker's pins
- Cotton threads (to match fabrics)
- Sewing machine
- Iron and ironing board
- Needle
- 250g (8oz) washable stuffing

FOR THE CLOTHES

- Fabrics (see patterns for quantity)
- 20cm (8in) narrow checked ribbon
- Pinking shears
- 80cm (32in) piece 5mm (¼in) wide elastic
- Safety pin
- 76cm (30in) rick-rack braid
- 30cm (12in) strip fasteners or velcro
- 41cm (16in) ribbon (colourful)
- 2 x 15mm (⅝in) self-cover buttons
- scraps felt (assorted colours)

FOR THE HAIR AND FACE

- 1 ball curly textured wool (black)
- 10cm (4in) bias binding (black)
- Fabric glue
- 11mm (⅜in) self-cover button
- Tailor's chalk
- Embroidery thread (red)
- Scraps felt (white, blue)

CUTTING OUT

BODY: plump doll's pattern pieces, pages 44-7
SHOES: plump doll's pattern piece, page 53
CLOTHES: pattern pieces, pages 62-5

◆ BODY ◆

Make up the body as on page 7.

◆ SHOES ◆

1 Make up the shoes as on page 10.
2 Hand stitch a small check ribbon bow onto each shoe.

◆ PANTALOONS ◆

1 Keep each piece of the pantaloons folded with the right sides facing and machine stitch along the inside leg with a 5mm (¼in) seam. Press the seams open.
2 Turn one leg piece right side out and place it inside the other, matching up the raw edges of the centre (crotch) seam. Machine stitch the two pieces together, again using a 5mm (¼in) seam. Press the seam flat and turn the inside leg out so that the garment is the wrong side out completely.
3 At the bottom of the legs, turn up 3cm (1¼in) on the ,inside to make a hem. Machine stitch a line 1cm (⅜in) from the bottom fold of the hem leaving a 12mm (½in) gap through which to insert the elastic, and then machine stitch another line 5mm (¼in) from the bottom fold. Trim the raw edges with pinking shears. Insert elastic into each casing using a safety pin to guide it. Gather to an appropriate size and stitch the ends of the elastic together cutting off the excess.
4 At the waist, turn over 3cm (1¼in) to the wrong side and machine stitch all around 1cm (⅜in) from the fold. Leave a 12mm (½in) gap through which to insert the elastic. Trim the raw edges with pinking shears and insert and finish off the elastic as for the bottom of the pantaloon legs.

◆ DRESS ◆

1 Machine stitch the dress front to the back pieces at the shoulders with a 5mm (¼in) seam. Press the seams flat.
2 Place the sleeves on the shoulders with the centre of the sleeve matching the centre seam of the shoulder and with the right sides facing. You might find it easier to baste the pieces together before machine stitching. Allow a 5mm (¼in) seam and press the seams open when finished.
3 On each cuff of the sleeve turn over 1cm

(⅜in) of fabric to the wrong side, press and then machine stitch in place. Do the same to the hem of the dress, adding a strip of rick-rack braid.
4 With right sides facing and starting at the end of each sleeve, sew up the side seam of the first sleeve and down the side of the dress allowing a 5mm (¼in) seam. Repeat on the other side. Press the seams open.
5 Press the neck seam over to neaten and machine stitch on a piece of rick-rack braid.
6 On each side at the back opening, turn over 2cm (¾in) to the wrong side , carefully press and machine stitch. Trim the raw edges with pinking shears.
7 To hold the dress closed, sew on a line of fasteners or a strip of velcro.
8 Tie four colourful ribbon bows and sew them onto the back opening of the dress (see photograph overleaf).
9 Cover the buttons with fabric and before you fasten them together attach a felt flower to the back. Sew the buttons onto the centre of her dress.

◆ HAIR ◆

1 Cut approximately 100 strands of wool. Lay the strands of wool evenly on a strip of similar-coloured bias binding and sew them down using either hand or machine stitch. If you have problems keeping the wool strands still while sewing you can always fasten them down with a dab of fabric glue.
2 Hand stitch the hair onto the head so that the parting lies in the centre. Use a similar coloured thread and small running stitches.

◆ FACE ◆

1 Follow Step 1 on page 10.
2 For the eyes cut two small oval shapes out of the white felt and stick them onto the face. Cut two smaller pieces of blue felt and stick them onto the white felt.

PARTY GIRLS - LITTLE SISTER

Here is a charmingly diminutive version of the Big Sister featured on the previous page. The photograph here shows her back which I really like because of the flamboyant ribbon bows; they are just right for party wear. Her Big Sister is dressed in just the same way down the back, but the details on their dresses are different.

YOU WILL NEED

FOR THE BODY

- 66 x 28cm (26 x 11in) brown felt
- Scissors
- Dressmaker's pins
- Cotton threads (to match fabrics)
- Sewing machine
- Iron and ironing board
- Needle
- 250g (8oz) washable stuffing

FOR THE CLOTHES

- Fabrics (see patterns for quantity)
- Pinking shears
- 61cm (24in) piece 5mm (¼in) wide elastic
- Safety pin
- 76cm (30in) rick-rack braid
- 20cm (8in) strip fasteners or velcro
- 41cm (16in) ribbon (colourful)
- 3 x 15mm (⅝in) self-cover buttons

FOR THE HAIR AND FACE

- 1 ball curly textured wool (black)
- 10cm (4in) bias binding (black)
- Fabric glue
- 10cm (4in) narrow ribbon
- 11mm (⅜in) self-cover button
- Tailor's chalk
- Embroidery thread (red)
- Scraps felt (white, blue)

CUTTING OUT

BODY: baby doll's pattern pieces, pages 51-2
SHOES: baby doll's pattern piece, page 53
CLOTHES: pattern pieces, pages 74-6

◆ BODY ◆

Make up the body as on page 7.

◆ SHOES ◆

1 Make up the shoes as on page 10.
2 Sew a small check ribbon bow onto each.

◆ PANTALOONS ◆

1 Keep each piece of the pantaloons folded with the right sides facing and machine stitch along the inside leg with a 5mm (¼in) seam. Press the seams open.
2 Turn one leg piece right side out and place it inside the other, matching up the raw edges of the centre (crotch) seam. Machine stitch the two pieces together, again using a 5mm (¼in) seam. Press the seam flat and turn the inside leg out so that the garment is the wrong side out completely.
3 At the bottom of the legs, turn up 2cm (⅜in) on the inside to make a hem. Machine stitch a line 1cm (⅜in) from the bottom fold of the hem leaving a 12mm (½in) gap through which to insert the elastic, and then machine stitch another line 5mm (¼in) from the bottom fold. Trim the raw edge with pinking shears. Insert a length of elastic into each casing using a safety pin to guide it. Gather the elastic to an appropriate size and stitch the ends together cutting off the excess.
4 At the waist, turn over 2cm (⅜in) to the wrong side and machine stitch all around 1cm (⅜in) from the fold. Leave a 12mm (½in) gap through which to insert the elastic. Trim the raw edges with pinking shears and insert and finish off the elastic as for the bottom of the pantaloon legs.

◆ DRESS ◆

1 Machine stitch the dress front to the back pieces at the shoulders with a 5mm (¼in) seam. Press the seams flat.
2 Place the sleeves on the shoulders with the centre of the sleeve matching the centre seam of the shoulder and with the right sides facing. You might find it easier to baste the pieces together before machine stitching. Allow a 5mm (¼in) seam and press the seams open when finished.
3 On each cuff of the sleeve turn over 1cm (⅜in) of fabric to the wrong side and press. Machine stitch in place adding rick-rack braid.

Do the same to the hem of the dress, also adding rick-rack braid.
4 With right sides facing and starting at the end of each sleeve, sew up the side seam of the first sleeve and down the side of the dress allowing a 5mm (¼in) seam. Repeat on the other side. Press the seams open.
5 Press the neck seam over to neaten and machine stitch on a piece of rick-rack braid.
6 On each side at the back opening, turn over 3cm (1¼in) to the wrong side and machine stitch. Trim the raw edges with pinking shears.
7 To hold the dress closed, sew on a line of fasteners or a strip of velcro.
8 Tie four colourful ribbon bows and sew them onto the back opening of the dress.
9 Cover the buttons with fabric and sew them onto the centre of her dress.

◆ HAIR ◆

1 Cut approximately 100 strands of wool. Lay the strands of wool evenly on a strip of similar-coloured bias binding and sew them down using either hand or machine stitch. If you have problems keeping the wool strands still while sewing you can always fasten them down with a dab of fabric glue.
2 Sew the hair onto the head so that the parting lies in the centre. Use a similar coloured thread and small running stitches.
3 Sew a small bow in her hair.

◆ FACE ◆

1 Cover the 11mm (⅜in) button with a piece of brown fabric and stitch it onto the face slightly below the centre.
2 Mark the shape of the mouth with a piece of tailor's chalk. Using red embroidery thread, stitch on the mouth.
3 For the eyes cut two small oval shapes out of the white felt and stick them onto the face. Cut two smaller pieces of blue felt and stick them onto the white felt.

INUIT

The icy elements and cold winds do not stand a chance of getting through this young Inuit's clothing. Enjoy collecting the different fabrics for the costume. As they are all white it is important to vary the textures so that each piece of clothing looks different.

YOU WILL NEED

FOR THE BODY

- 31 x 100cm (12 x 39in) calico or cotton
- 18 x 40cm (7 x 16in) cotton jersey
- Scissors
- Dressmaker's pins
- Cotton threads (to match fabrics)
- Sewing machine
- Iron and ironing board
- Needle
- 250g (8oz) washable stuffing

FOR THE CLOTHES

- Fabrics (see patterns for quantity)
- Pinking shears
- 41cm (16in) piece 5mm (¼in) wide elastic
- Safety pin
- 18cm (7in) fasteners or velcro
- 8 pompoms (white)
- 20cm (8in) strip white feathers or fur

FOR THE FACE

- 11mm (⅜in) self-cover button
- Tailor's chalk
- Embroidery threads (red, yellow)
- Scrap felt (black)
- Fabric glue

CUTTING OUT

BODY: plump doll's pattern pieces, pages 44-7
SHOES: plump doll's pattern piece, page 53
CLOTHES: pattern pieces, pages 70-3

◆ BODY ◆

Make up the body using the plump doll pattern on pages 44-7 and following the instructions on page 7.

◆ SHOES ◆

1 Carefully cut out four pieces of fabric from the pattern.
2 Fold the top edge of each shoe over by 5mm (¼in) and machine stitch down.
3 Machine stitch each shoe together with right sides facing. Press the seams open and turn right sides out.

◆ TROUSERS ◆

1 Keep each piece of the trousers folded with the right sides facing and machine stitch along the inside leg with a 5mm (¼in) seam. Press the seams open.
2 Turn one leg piece right side out and place it inside the other, matching up the raw edges of the centre (crotch) seam. Machine stitch the two pieces together, again using a 5mm (¼in) seam. Press the seam flat and turn the inside leg out so that the garment is the wrong side out completely.
3 At the bottom of the legs, turn up 1cm (⅜in) of fabric to make a hem and machine stitch along this hem line.
4 At the waist, turn over 3cm (1¼in) to the wrong side and machine stitch all around, 1cm (⅜in) from the fold and leaving a 12mm (½in) gap through which to insert the elastic. Trim the raw edges with pinking shears. Insert a length of elastic into the casing using a safety pin to guide it. Gather to an appropriate size and stitch the ends of the elastic together cutting off the excess.

◆ JACKET ◆

1 Machine stitch the shirt front to the back pieces at the shoulders with a 5mm (¼in) seam. Press the seams flat.
2 Place the sleeves on the shoulders with the centre of the sleeve matching the centre seam of the shoulder and with the right sides facing. You might find it easier to baste the pieces together before machine stitching. Allow a 5mm (¼in) seam and press the seams open when finished.
3 On each cuff, turn over 1cm (⅜in) to the wrong side and machine stitch. Do the same to each open side of the jacket and the hem. Trim the raw edges with pinking shears.
4 With right sides facing and starting at the end of each sleeve, sew up the side seam of the first sleeve and down the side of the shirt allowing a 5mm (¼in) seam. Repeat on the other side. Press the seams open.
5 Press the neck seam over to neaten and machine stitch.
6 On each side at the back opening, turn over 2cm (¾in) to the wrong side and machine stitch. Trim the raw edges with pinking shears.
7 To hold the shirt closed, sew on a line of fasteners or a strip of velcro.
8 Sew white pompoms right around the hem of the jacket.

◆ HOOD ◆

1 Fold the fabric in half with right sides facing. Sew along the curved edge (marked on the pattern a-b), allowing a 5mm (¼in) seam.
2 Move this seam across so that it is placed on top of the back fold. The top left-hand corner right angle will not be a straight line. Machine stitch along this seam, allowing a 5mm (¼in) seam.
3 Turn the hood right side out. Turn over 1cm (⅜in) of all the raw edges to the wrong side of the hood and press.
4 Pin and baste the edges of the hood onto the jacket and machine stitch around. Fold back the front edge of the hood on the wrong side of the fabric so that it lines up with the rest of the jacket and machine stitch in place.
5 Sew a strip of feathers or fur around the rim of the hood.
6 Sew a line of fasteners down the front of the jacket to hold it together.

◆ FACE ◆

1 Cover the 11mm (⅜in) button with a piece of the face fabric and stitch onto the face, slightly below the centre.
2 Mark the shape of the mouth with a piece of tailor's chalk. Using red embroidery thread, stitch on the mouth.
3 For the eyes, cut two small circles out of the black felt and stick them onto the face. Sew small yellow lines of embroidery thread to indicate eyelashes.

NATIVE AMERICAN DOLL

O ne of the most exciting parts of making up this doll's outfit is being creative with her headdress for this is the focal point of the traditional costume. Hand embroider the headband with colourful and simple stitches, such as running stitch and cross stitch.

YOU WILL NEED

FOR THE BODY

- 46 x 46cm (18 x 18in) calico or cotton
- 18 x 36cm (7 x 14in) cotton jersey
- Scissors
- Dressmaker's pins
- Cotton threads (to match fabrics)
- Sewing machine
- Iron and ironing board
- Needle
- 250g (8oz) washable stuffing

FOR THE CLOTHES

- Fabrics (see patterns for quantity)
- Pinking shears
- 85cm (34in) piece 5mm (¼in) wide elastic
- Safety pin
- 76cm (30in) suede fringing (black, tan)
- Fabric glue
- Embroidery threads (assorted colours)
- 18cm (7in) strip fasteners or velcro

FOR THE HAIR, HEADDRESS AND FACE

- 1 ball wool (brown)
- 10cm (4in) bias binding (brown)
- Wooden beads (assorted colours)
- 30 x 3cm (12 x 1¼in) coloured band
- Tailor's chalk
- Feathers
- 11mm (⅜in) self-cover button
- Scrap felt (black)

CUTTING OUT

BODY: thin doll's pattern pieces, pages 48-50
CLOTHES AND SHOES: pattern pieces, pages 77-9; plus pantaloons on pages 54-5 and shirt front, back and sleeves on pages 60-1

◆ BODY ◆

Make up the body as on page 7.

◆ SHOES ◆

Make up the shoes as on page 10.

◆ PANTALOONS ◆

Make up the pantaloons as on page 10.

◆ SKIRT ◆

1 With the right sides facing, sew the two pieces of fabric together along the side seams, allowing a 5mm (¼in) seam. Press open.
2 At the waist, turn over 3cm (1¼in) to the wrong side and machine stitch all around 1cm (⅜in) from the fold leaving a 12mm (½in) gap. Trim the raw edges with pinking shears. Insert a length of elastic as for the pantaloons.
3 At the skirt hem, turn over 1cm (⅜in) to the wrong side and press. Baste or glue a piece of suede fringing on the right side of the hem and machine stitch.
4 Hand sew a line of running stitch just above the fringing in a colourful embroidery thread.

◆ SHIRT ◆

1 Machine stitch the shirt front to the back pieces at the shoulders with a 5mm (¼in) seam. Press the seams flat.
2 Place the sleeves on the shoulders with the centre of the sleeve matching the centre seam of the shoulder and with the right sides facing. You might find it easier to baste the pieces together before machine stitching. Allow a 5mm (¼in) seam and press the seams open when finished.
3 On each cuff of the sleeve, turn over 1cm (⅜in) of fabric to the wrong side and machine stitch. Do the same at the hem.
4 With right sides facing and starting at the end of each sleeve, sew up the side seam of the first sleeve and down the side of the shirt allowing a 5mm (¼in) seam. Repeat on the other side. Press the seams open. Press the neck seam over to neaten and machine stitch.
5 On each side at the back opening, turn over 2cm (¾in) to the wrong side and machine stitch. Trim the raw edges with pinking shears.
6 To hold the shirt closed, sew on a line of fasteners or a strip of velcro.

◆ WAISTCOAT ◆

1 Machine stitch the waistcoat back to the two front pieces at the shoulders with a 5mm (¼in) seam. Press the seams flat.
2 Machine stitch the sides of the waistcoat with a 5mm (¼in) in seam.
3 At the hem and neck lines, turn over 1cm (⅜in), clipping into the curves if necessary, and machine stitch. Trim the raw edges with pinking shears. Carefully machine stitch a piece of suede fringing all around the hem of the waistcoat.
4 Using colourful embroidery threads, hand sew lines of running stitch along the edges of the waistcoat.

◆ HAIR ◆

1 Make up the hair following Steps 1 to 3 on page 10.
2 Divide the hair into two bunches and plait them three-quarters of the way down. Fasten them with a piece of the same coloured wool. Thread small colourful beads onto the hair at the end of each plait tying a knot at the ends of the wool to secure them.

◆ HEADDRESS ◆

1 Place the band around the head so that you can see where to place the feathers. Mark the section with a piece of tailor's chalk.
2 Baste the feathers in place on one side of the band and then machine or hand stitch depending on how tough they are.
3 Decorate the band with colourful hand stitches, such as running and cross stitch.
4 Place the headdress around the head. At the back, cross the ends over and secure with a cross stitch. Hand stitch the rest of the headdress onto the doll's head with small running stitches in a similar coloured cotton thread to keep it in place.

◆ FACE ◆

Make up the face as on page 10 but use black embroidery thread in place of yellow embroidery thread for the eyelashes.

CENTRAL AMERICAN DOLL

Colour is the essential ingredient of this doll's costume. Combine rich and vibrant fabrics with patterned and textured braids to create an overall feeling of warmth. Try to use bright, interesting fabrics for all the layers of clothing, especially the poncho.

YOU WILL NEED

FOR THE BODY

- 31 x 100cm (12 x 39in) calico or cotton
- 18 x 40cm (7 x 16in) cotton jersey
- Dressmaker's pins
- Cotton threads (to match fabrics)
- Sewing machine
- Iron and ironing board
- Needle
- 250g (8oz) washable stuffing

FOR THE CLOTHES

- Fabrics (see patterns for quantity)
- Pinking shears
- 1.2m (4ft) piece 5mm (¼in) wide elastic
- Safety pin
- 18cm (7in) strip fasteners or velcro
- 1.2m (4ft) decorative trimmings and braids
- 90cm (36in) pompom trimming

FOR THE HAIR AND FACE

- 1 ball wool (brown)
- Strips of coloured fabric
- 10cm (4in) bias binding (brown)
- Fabric glue
- 25cm (10in) ribbon
- 11mm (⅜in) self-cover button
- Tailor's chalk
- Embroidery threads (red, black)
- Scrap felt (black)
- Coloured chalk or make-up blusher

CUTTING OUT

BODY: plump doll's pattern pieces, pages 44-7
SHOES: plump doll's pattern piece, page 53
CLOTHES: pattern pieces, pages 80-5; plus pantaloons on pages 62-3

◆ BODY ◆

Make up the body as on page 7.

◆ SHOES ◆

Make up the shoes as on page 10.

◆ PANTALOONS ◆

Make up the pantaloons as on page 10.

◆ SKIRT ◆

1 With the right sides facing, sew the fabric pieces together along the side seams, allowing a 5mm (¼in) seam. Press the seam open.
2 At the waist, turn over 3cm (1¼in) to the wrong side and machine stitch all around 1cm (⅜in) from the fold leaving a 12mm (½in) gap. Trim the raw edges with pinking shears. Insert a length of elastic as for the pantaloons.
3 At the skirt hem, turn over 1cm (⅜in) to the wrong side and press.

◆ SHIRT ◆

1 Machine stitch the shirt front to the back pieces at the shoulders with a 5mm (¼in) seam. Press the seams flat.
2 Place the sleeves on the shoulders with the centre of the sleeve matching the centre seam of the shoulder and with the right sides facing. You might find it easier to baste the pieces together before machine stitching. Allow a 5mm (¼in) seam and press the seams open when finished.
3 On each cuff of the sleeve, turn over 1cm (⅜in) of fabric to the wrong side and machine stitch. Do the same at the hem.
4 With right sides facing and starting at the end of each sleeve, sew up the side seam of the first sleeve and down the side of the shirt allowing a 5mm (¼in) seam. Repeat on the other side. Press the seams open.
5 Press the neck seam over to neaten and machine stitch.
6 On each side at the back opening, turn over 2cm (¾in) to the wrong side and machine stitch. Trim the raw edges with pinking shears.
7 To hold the shirt closed, sew on a line of fasteners or a strip of velcro.

◆ PONCHO ◆

1 Sew the two back parts of the poncho to the front with a 5mm (¼in) seam. Press the seams open.
2 On each side at the back opening, turn over 2cm (¾in) to the wrong side and machine stitch in place. Trim the raw edges with pinking shears.
3 Press the neck seam over to neaten and sew on a piece of decorative ribbon.
4 Turn the hem under 1cm (⅜in) and press. Baste on strips of pompom trimming and braid around the hem and machine stitch in place.
5 To hold the poncho closed, sew on a line of fasteners or a strip of velcro.

◆ HAIR ◆

1 Cut approximately 150 strands of wool and four strips of fabric each the same length (this is only a guideline as it is up to you how thick and long you wish to make the hair). Lay the centre of the strands of wool and fabric evenly on a strip of similar-coloured bias binding and then sew them down using either hand or machine stitch. If you have problems in keeping the wool strands still while sewing you can always fasten them down with a dab of fabric glue.
2 Sew the hair onto the head, so that the parting lies in the centre of the head. Use a similar coloured thread and make small, neat running stitches.
3 Divide the hair neatly into two bunches and plait them. Then tie a ribbon at the end of each plait.

◆ FACE ◆

1 Cover the 11mm (⅜in) button with a piece of the face fabric and stitch onto the face, slightly below the centre.
2 Mark the shape of the mouth with a piece of tailor's chalk. Using red embroidery thread, stitch on the mouth.
3 For the eyes, cut two small circles out of the black felt and stick them onto the face. Sew small black lines of embroidery thread to indicate eyelashes.
4 Using the coloured chalk or make-up blusher, give the doll some rosy cheeks.

FANCY DRESS DOLLS

It's party time. Here are seven dolls dressed in fancy dress attire for a touch of fantasy play. Ranging from a wicked pirate complete with earring and patch to a gentle fairy with her resplendent wings and wand, there are complete making instructions for each rag doll on the following pages.

WICKED PIRATE

This adventurous doll is dressed for an exciting and mysterious voyage across the ocean, where no doubt he is on a mission to discover hidden treasures. I've decorated his outfit with a trimming of gold braid and gold buttons to give him an air of extravagance. However, the eye patch and solitary earring make us aware that he is still very devious and secretive.

YOU WILL NEED

FOR THE BODY
- 46 x 46cm (18 x 18in) calico or cotton
- 18 x 36cm (7 x 14in) cotton jersey
- Dressmaker's pins
- Cotton threads (to match fabrics)
- Sewing machine
- Iron and ironing board
- Needle
- 250g (8oz) washable stuffing

FOR THE CLOTHES
- Fabrics (see patterns for quantity)
- Pinking shears
- 50cm (20in) piece 5mm (¼in) wide elastic
- Safety pin
- 30cm (12in) satin ribbon (black)
- Small brass buckle
- 20in (8cm) strip fasteners or velcro
- Braid (gold)
- 2 gold buttons
- 30cm (12in) braid (gold)
- 30cm (12in) cord elastic (black)

FOR THE FACE
- 11mm (⅜in) self-cover button
- Scrap felt (black)
- Fabric glue
- Embroidery thread (red)
- Gold hoop

CUTTING OUT
BODY: thin doll's pattern pieces, pages 48-50
SHOES: pointed pattern piece, page 53
CLOTHES: pattern pieces, pages 86-7; plus shirt front, back and sleeves on pages 60-1

◆ BODY ◆
Make up the body as on page 7.

◆ SHOES ◆
Make up the shoes as on page 10.

◆ PANTALOONS ◆
1 Make up the pantaloons following Steps 1 to 3 described on page 10.

2 At the waist, turn over 3cm (1¼in) to the wrong side and machine stitch all around 1cm (⅜in) from the fold. Leave a 12mm (½in) gap through which to insert the elastic. Trim the raw edges with pinking shears and insert and finish off the elastic as for the bottom of the pantaloon legs.

3 For the belt, cut the satin ribbon to fit around the waist and thread it through the buckle. To fasten the loose ends of the belt around the body, sew a fastener or a small piece of velcro onto the ends of the ribbon.

◆ SHIRT ◆
1 Machine stitch the shirt front to the back pieces at the shoulders with a 5mm (¼in) seam. Press the seams flat.

2 Place the sleeves on the shoulders with the centre of the sleeve matching the centre seam of the shoulder and with the right sides facing. You might find it easier to baste the pieces together before machine stitching. Allow a 5mm (¼in) seam and press the seams open when finished.

3 On each cuff of the sleeve, turn over 1cm (⅜in) of fabric to the wrong side, press carefully and machine stitch. Do the same at the hem.

4 With right sides facing and starting at the end of each sleeve, sew up the side seam of the first sleeve and down the side of the shirt allowing a 5mm (¼in) seam. Repeat on the other side. Press the seams open.

5 Press the neck seam over to neaten and machine stitch.

6 On each side at the back opening, turn over 2cm (⅜in) to the wrong side and machine stitch. Trim the raw edges with pinking shears.

7 To hold the shirt closed, sew on a line of fasteners or a strip of velcro.

8 Sew two gold buttons in a line on the front of the shirt.

◆ WAISTCOAT ◆
1 Machine stitch the waistcoat back to the two front pieces at the shoulders with a 5mm (¼in) seam. Press the seams flat.

2 Machine stitch the sides of the waistcoat with a 5mm (¼in) seam. Carefully press the seams open.

3 Turn the edges under around the arm by 1cm (⅜in), clipping into the curves if necessary, and machine stitch. Do the same to the rest of the waistcoat.

4 Hand stitch a piece of gold braid around the bottom edge.

◆ SCARF ◆
1 With right sides facing, machine stitch the two pieces of fabric together, leaving a gap for turning right sides out.

2 Turn the scarf right sides out, over stitch the opening to close and press. Top stitch around the edge.

◆ EYE PATCH ◆
1 Measure around the head to find out the length of elastic you will need. Trap the ends of the elastic between the black felt shapes at either side and machine stitch around the black felt.

◆ FACE ◆
1 Cover the 11mm (⅜in) button with a piece of the face fabric and stitch onto the face, slightly below the centre.

2 Cut out the moustache from the black felt and stick it in position on the face using the fabric glue.

3 Sew a few red lines under the moustache to indicate the mouth.

4 Cut out a small black circle of felt for the visible eye and glue it onto the face, again using the fabric glue.

5 Sew the small gold hoop onto the left side of the face.

FAIRY

Create your own fantastical, sparkly fairy by using shiny white fabrics and glittery bits and pieces. Make her outfit look pure and special in the hope that she will twinkle her wand bringing you good luck. Sew a glitzy pompom onto the tip of each toe for added sparkle.

YOU WILL NEED

FOR THE BODY

- 46 x 46cm (18 x 18in) calico or cotton
- 18 x 36cm (7 x 14in) cotton jersey
- Scissors
- Dressmaker's pins
- Cotton threads (to match fabrics, silver)
- Sewing machine
- Iron and ironing board
- Needle
- 250g (8oz) washable stuffing

FOR THE CLOTHES

- Fabrics (see patterns for quantity)
- 2 pompoms (silver)
- Pinking shears
- 81cm (32in) piece 5mm (¼in) wide elastic
- Safety pin
- 36cm (14in) fringing (silver)
- 61cm (24in) rick-rack braid (silver)
- 30cm (12in) strip fasteners or velcro
- 25 x 20cm (10 x 8in) stiff iron-on interfacing
- Fabric glue
- 20cm (8in) cord elastic (silver)

FOR THE HAIR, FACE AND WAND

- 1 ball wool (silver)
- 10cm (4in) bias binding (silver)
- 11mm (⅜in) self-cover button
- Tailor's chalk
- Embroidery thread (pink, yellow)
- Scrap felt (blue)
- Silver card
- 30cm (12in) satin-covered wire
- Strong glue

CUTTING OUT

BODY: thin doll's pattern pieces, pages 48-50
SHOES: thin doll's pattern piece, page 53
CLOTHES: pattern pieces, pages 88-9; plus pantaloons on pages 54-5 and dress front, back and sleeves on pages 54-7

◆ BODY ◆

Make up the body following the instructions on page 7.

◆ SHOES ◆

1 Make up the shoes as on page 10.
2 Hand stitch a silver pompom onto the tip of each shoe.

◆ PANTALOONS ◆

Make up the pantaloons as on page 10.

◆ DRESS ◆

1 Machine stitch the dress front to the back pieces at the shoulders with a 5mm (¼in) seam. Press the seams flat.
2 Place the sleeves on the shoulders with the centre of the sleeve matching the centre seam of the shoulder and with the right sides facing. You might find it easier to baste the pieces together before machine stitching. Allow a 5mm (¼in) seam and press the seams open when finished.
3 With right sides facing and starting at the end of each sleeve, sew up the side seam of the first sleeve and down the side of the dress allowing a 5mm (¼in) seam. Repeat on the other side. Press the seams open.
4 On each cuff turn over 1cm (⅜in) of fabric to the wrong side and press. Sew on a piece of silver fringing. Do the same to the hem of the dress using rick-rack braid.
5 Press the neck seam over to neaten and machine stitch in place.
6 On each side at the back opening, turn over 2cm (¾in) to the wrong side and machine stitch. Trim the raw edges with pinking shears.
7 To hold the dress closed, sew on a line of fasteners or a strip of velcro.
8 Using silver thread, hand stitch stars over the main body of the dress.

◆ WINGS ◆

1 Iron the interfacing onto the reverse side of one fabric piece of each wing.
2 With the wrong sides facing, sew the wings together with a 5mm (¼in) seam, leaving a small gap for turning.

3 Turn right sides out, over stitch the opening to close and press. Cut around the edge with pinking shears.
4 Stick a star cut from some silver fabric on each side of the wing with fabric glue.
5 Sew a length of silver cord elastic through the top and bottom of the straight edge of each wing, forming a loop. Place the loop around the arm and once you have checked that the elastic is tight enough to support the wings, tie a knot to fasten.

◆ HAIR ◆

1 Cut approximately 150 strands of silver wool and centre them evenly on a piece of similar-coloured bias binding. Machine or hand stitch them down. If you have problems keeping the wool strands still while sewing you can always fasten them down with a dab of fabric glue.
2 Sew the hair onto the head so that the parting lies in the centre of the head. Use a similar-coloured thread and suitably small, neat running stitches.
3 Divide the hair into two even bunches and plait them. Secure the ends by tying a piece of the same wool around them.
4 Starting from the top, coil the plait around to form a bun, pinning in place as you go. Secure each by hand stitching to the head.
5 To finish off, sew or glue three strands of the silver wool across the parting.

◆ FACE ◆

1 Follow Step 1 on page 10.
2 For the eyes, cut two small circles out of the blue felt and stick them onto the face. Sew small yellow lines of embroidery thread to indicate eyelashes.

◆ WAND ◆

1 Cut out two stars from silver card.
2 Trap a satin-covered piece of wire between the two stars and glue to secure.

WIZARD

Wizards and witches (see overleaf) are wise characters full of secret spells and tricks. To create a magical, twinkling quality to the wizard's costume I have coordinated shiny fabrics. If you can't find a fabric with stars, use fabric paints to paint your own.

YOU WILL NEED

FOR THE BODY
- 46 x 46cm (18 x 18in) calico or cotton
- 18 x 36cm (7 x 14in) cotton jersey
- Scissors
- Dressmaker's pins
- Cotton threads (to match fabrics)
- Sewing machine
- Iron
- Ironing board
- Needle
- 250g (8oz) washable stuffing

FOR THE CLOTHES
- Fabrics (see patterns for quantity)
- Pinking shears
- 61cm (24in) piece 5mm (¼in) wide elastic
- Safety pin
- 36cm (14in) strip fasteners or velcro
- 20cm (8in) narrow ribbon (red)

FOR THE HAIR, HAT AND FACE
- 1 ball wool (grey)
- 10cm (4in) bias binding (grey)
- Fabric glue
- 20 x 30cm (8 x 12in) felt (red)
- Star sequins (silver)
- 11mm (⅜in) self-cover button
- Scrap felt (black)

CUTTING OUT

BODY: thin doll's pattern pieces, pages 48-50
SHOES: pointed pattern piece, page 53
CLOTHES: pattern pieces, pages 90-3; plus pantaloons on pages 54-5 and dress (robe) front, back and sleeves on pages 54-7

◆ BODY ◆
Make up the body as on page 7.

◆ SHOES ◆
Make up the shoes as on page 10.

◆ PANTALOONS ◆
1 Keep each piece of the pantaloons folded with the right sides facing and machine stitch

along the inside leg with a 5mm (¼in) seam. Press the seams open.
2 Turn one leg piece right side out and place it inside the other, matching up the raw edges of the centre (crotch) seam. Machine stitch the two pieces together, again using a 5mm (¼in) seam. Press the seam flat and turn the inside leg out so that the garment is the wrong side out completely.
3 At the bottom of the legs, turn up 3cm (1¼in) on the inside to make a hem. Machine stitch a line 15mm (⅝in) from the bottom fold of the hem leaving a 12mm (½in) gap through which to insert the elastic, and then machine stitch another line 5mm (¼in) from the bottom fold. Trim the raw edges with pinking shears. Insert elastic into each casing using a safety pin to guide it. Gather to an appropriate size and stitch the ends of the elastic together cutting off the excess.
4 At the waist, turn over 3cm (1¼in) to the wrong side and machine stitch all around 1cm (⅜in) from the fold. Leave a 12mm (½in) gap through which to insert the elastic. Trim the raw edges with pinking shears and insert and finish off the elastic as for the legs.

◆ ROBE ◆
1 Machine stitch the robe front to the back pieces at the shoulders with a 5mm (¼in) seam. Press the seams flat.
2 Place the sleeves on the shoulders with the centre matching the centre seam of the shoulder and with the right sides facing. You might find it easier to baste the pieces together before machine stitching. Allow a 5mm (¼in) seam; press open when finished.
3 On each cuff of the sleeves and the hem, turn over 1cm (⅜in) of fabric to the wrong side and machine stitch in place.
4 With right sides facing and starting at the end of each sleeve, sew up the side seam of the first sleeve and down the side of the robe allowing a 5mm (¼in) seam. Repeat on the

other side. Press the seams open.
5 Press the neck seam over to neaten and machine stitch in place.
6 On each side at the back opening, turn over 2cm (¾in) to the wrong side and machine stitch. Trim the raw edges with pinking shears.
7 To hold the robe closed, sew on a line of fasteners or a strip of velcro.

◆ CLOAK ◆
1 With right sides facing, sew the two front parts of the cloak to the back with a 5mm (¼in) seam allowance. Press the seams open.
2 On each side at the front opening, turn over 1cm (⅜in) to the wrong side and machine stitch. Trim the raw edges with pinking shears. Do the same to the hem of the cloak.
3 Turn the collar of the cloak over 3cm (1¼in) to the wrong side and press. Machine stitch a line 2cm (¾in) from the fold. Sew another line 2.5cm (1in) from the fold. Trim the raw edges with pinking shears.
4 Thread the narrow ribbon through the tube.

◆ HAIR AND BEARD ◆
1 Make up the hair following Steps 1 and 2 on page 16.
2 Cut approximately ten strands of wool and tie a piece of wool around the centre. Stitch the bundle onto the face and trim to create a pointed look.

◆ HAT ◆
1 With right sides facing, sew the two pieces of felt together along the long seam.
2 Turn right sides out and then sew gold star-shaped sequins over the hat.

◆ FACE ◆
1 Cover the 11mm (⅜in) button with a piece of the face fabric and stitch onto the face, slightly below the centre.
2 For the eyes, cut two small circles out of the black felt and stick them onto the face.

WITCH

Although the witch's costume is predominately black, it is important to use different textured fabrics to vary the overall tone. I've embellished her robe with silver fabric moons which are glued on; these give her an extra sparkle.

YOU WILL NEED

FOR THE BODY
- 46 x 46cm (18 x 18in) calico or cotton
- 18 x 36cm (7 x 14in) cotton jersey
- Dressmaker's pins
- Cotton threads (to match fabrics)
- Sewing machine
- Iron and ironing board
- Needle
- 250g (8oz) washable stuffing

FOR THE CLOTHES
- Fabrics (see patterns for quantity)
- Pinking shears
- 76cm (30in) piece 5mm (¼in) wide elastic
- Safety pin
- 36cm (14in) strip fasteners or velcro
- 20cm (8in) fringing (black)
- Embroidery threads (black, red)
- 4 beads (black)
- 20cm (8in) narrow ribbon (black)

FOR THE HAIR, HAT AND FACE
- 1 ball wool (black)
- 10cm (4in) bias binding (black)
- Fabric glue
- 20 x 30cm (8 x 12in) felt (black)
- 11mm (⅜in) self-cover button
- Tailor's chalk
- Scrap felt (black)

CUTTING OUT

BODY: thin doll's pattern pieces, pages 48-50
SHOES: pointed pattern piece, page 53
CLOTHES: pattern pieces, pages 90-3; plus pantaloons on pages 54-5 and dress (robe) front, back and sleeves on pages 54-7

◆ BODY ◆
Make up the body as on page 7.

◆ SHOES ◆
Make up the shoes as on page 10.

◆ PANTALOONS ◆
Make up the pantaloons as on page 10.

◆ ROBE ◆
1 Machine stitch the robe front to the back pieces at the shoulders with a 5mm (¼in) seam. Press the seam flat.
2 Place the sleeves on the shoulders with the centre of the sleeve matching the centre seam of the shoulder and with the right sides facing. You might find it easier to baste the pieces together before machine stitching. Allow a 5mm (¼in) seam and press the seams open when finished.
3 On each cuff of the sleeves, turn over 1cm (⅜in) of fabric to the wrong side, carefully press and machine stitch in place. Do the same to the hem of the robe.
4 With right sides facing and starting at the end of each sleeve, sew up the side seam of the first sleeve and down the side of the robe allowing a 5mm (¼in) seam. Repeat on the other side. Press the seams open.
5 Press the neck seam over to neaten and machine stitch in place.
6 On each side at the back opening, turn over 2cm (¾in) to the wrong side and machine stitch. Trim the raw edges with pinking shears.
7 To hold the robe closed, sew on a line of fasteners or a strip of velcro.

◆ CLOAK ◆
1 With right sides facing, sew the two front parts of the cloak to the back with a 5mm (¼in) seam allowance. Press the seams open.
2 On each side at the front opening, turn over 1cm (⅜in) to the wrong side and machine stitch. Trim the raw edges with pinking shears. Do the same to the hem of the cloak.
3 Turn the collar of the cloak over 3cm (1¼in) to the wrong side and press. Machine stitch a line 2cm (¾in) from the fold. Sew another line 2.5cm (1in) from the fold. Trim the raw edges with pinking shears.
4 Sew a piece of black fringing along the top edge of the collar and embroider a spider on a corner of the cloak, using two of the beads to

make the spider's bright eyes.
5 Thread the ribbon through the tube again using the saftey pin as a guide.

◆ HAIR ◆
1 Cut approximately 100 strands of wool for the main hair (this is only a guideline as it is up to you how thick and long you wish to make the hair). Lay the centre of the strands of wool evenly on a strip of similar-coloured bias binding and sew them down using either hand or machine stitch. If you have problems keeping the wool strands still while sewing you can always fasten them down with a dab of fabric glue.
2 For the fringe, cut approximately 50 strands to the same length as the main hair. Lay the strands of wool on another strip of bias binding. The bias binding should lie approximately 5cm (2in) from one end of the strands. Again secure the strands using hand or machine stitch.
3 To attach the hair to the doll's head, first sew down the fringe piece, with the strip of bias binding running over the top of the head from side to side. Do this using a similar coloured thread and small running stitches. Then attach the main hair piece so that it runs at right angles to the other piece, forming a parting in the middle. Trim your doll's hair to the desired length.

◆ HAT ◆
1 With right sides facing, sew the two pieces of felt together along the long seam. Turn right sides out.
2 Hand sew a spider onto the front of the hat using a simple running stitch and sewing on two beads for the eyes.

◆ FACE ◆
Make up the face as on page 10 but use black embroidery thread in place of yellow embroidery thread for the eyelashes.

SAILOR BOY

This smartly dressed sailor would be an asset to any sailing crew. In his pristine uniform, he is set to sail across the far and open seas. His smart navy blue collar has white lines stitched onto it for some accurate detailing.

YOU WILL NEED

FOR THE BODY

- 46 x 46cm (18 x 18in) calico or cotton
- 18 x 36cm (7 x 14in) cotton jersey
- Dressmaker's pins
- Cotton threads (to match fabrics)
- Sewing machine
- Iron and ironing board
- Needle
- 250g (8oz) washable stuffing

FOR THE CLOTHES

- Fabrics (see patterns for quantity)
- Pinking shears
- 50cm (20in) piece 5mm (¼in) wide elastic
- Safety pin
- Embroidery threads (blue, red)
- 25cm (10in) ribbon (blue)
- 18cm (7in) fasteners or velcro
- 10cm (4in) narrow ribbon (white)

FOR THE HAIR AND FACE

- 1 ball wool (black)
- 11mm (⅜in) self-cover button
- Tailor's chalk
- Scrap felt (black)
- Fabric glue

CUTTING OUT

BODY: thin doll's pattern pieces, pages 48-50
SHOES: thin doll's pattern piece, page 53
CLOTHES: pattern piece, page 94; plus trousers on pages 58-9 and shirt front, back and sleeves on pages 60-1

◆ BODY ◆

Make up the body as on page 7.

◆ SHOES ◆

1 Carefully cut out four pieces of fabric from the pattern.
2 Fold the top edge of each shoe over by 5mm (¼in) and machine stitch down.
3 Machine stitch each shoe together with right sides facing. Press the seams open and turn right sides out.

◆ TROUSERS ◆

1 Keep each piece of the trousers folded with the right sides facing and machine stitch along the inside leg with a 5mm (¼in) seam. Press the seams open.
2 Turn one leg piece right side out and place it inside the other, matching up the raw edges of the centre (crotch) seam. Machine stitch the two pieces together, again using a 5mm (¼in) seam. Press the seam flat and turn the inside leg out so that the garment is the wrong side out completely.
3 At the bottom of the legs, turn up 1cm (⅜in) of fabric to make a hem and machine stitch along this hem line.
4 At the waist, turn over 3cm (1¼in) to the wrong side and machine stitch all around, 1cm (⅜in) from the fold and leaving a 12mm (½in) gap through which to insert the elastic. Trim the raw edges with pinking shears. Insert a length of elastic into the casing using a safety pin to guide it. Gather to an appropriate size and stitch the ends of the elastic together cutting off the excess.
5 Hand sew two lines of running stitch using the blue embroidery thread around each leg hem to decorate.

◆ SHIRT ◆

1 Machine stitch the shirt front to the back pieces at the shoulders with a 5mm (¼in) seam. Press the seams flat.
2 Place the sleeves on the shoulders with the centre of the sleeve matching the centre seam of the shoulder and with the right sides facing. You might find it easier to baste the pieces together before machine stitching. Allow a 5mm (¼in) seam and press the seams open when finished.
3 On each cuff, turn over 1cm (⅜in) of fabric and machine stitch. Machine stitch a piece of blue ribbon around each cuff.
4 With right sides facing and starting at the end of each sleeve, sew up the side seam of

the first sleeve and down the side of the shirt allowing a 5mm (¼in) seam. Repeat on the other side. Press the seams open.
5 Press the neck seam over to neaten and machine stitch.
6 On each side at the back opening, turn over 2cm (¾in) to the wrong side and machine stitch. Trim the raw edges with pinking shears.
7 To hold the shirt closed, sew on a line of fasteners or a strip of velcro.
8 Sew a line of running stitches around the hem of the shirt.

◆ COLLAR ◆

1 Machine or hand stitch along the marked lines with white thread.
2 Gather each length of the collar where marked on the pattern by gently pulling up lines of running stitch.
3 Place the collar around the sailor's neck and position the two ties over each other. To secure, stitch a fastening under the front tie. Sew on a small white ribbon in a bow where the ties meet.

◆ HAIR ◆

1 Cut approximately 100 strands of wool all the same length and tie a piece of wool around the centre of them. Pull it tight and knot firmly in place.
2 Hand sew the knot onto the top of the head and arrange the hair to create a style, trimming as necessary.

◆ FACE ◆

1 Cover the 11mm (⅜in) button with a piece of the face fabric and stitch onto the face, slightly below the centre.
2 Mark the shape of the mouth with a piece of tailor's chalk. Using red embroidery thread, stitch on the mouth.
3 For the eyes, cut two small circles out of the black felt and stick them onto the face using the fabric glue.

CIRCUS GIRL

This girl's cheeky grin and colourful clothes will brighten up the life of anyone looking for a cuddly companion. I've used contrasting colours to attract the eye, but kept to matching patterns for a touch of class. The curly rick-rack braid and pompom trim on my Circus Girl's dress add to the atmosphere of all the fun of the fair.

YOU WILL NEED
FOR THE BODY
- 31 x 100cm (12 x 39in) calico or cotton
- 18 x 40cm (7 x 16in) cotton jersey
- Scissors
- Dressmaker's pins
- Cotton threads (to match fabrics)
- Sewing machine
- Iron and ironing board
- Needle
- 250g (8oz) washable stuffing

FOR THE CLOTHES
- Fabrics (see patterns for quantity)
- Pinking shears
- 81cm (32in) piece 5mm (¼in) wide elastic
- Safety pin
- 10 ribbon roses
- 1.1m (43in) rick-rack braid
- Fabric glue
- 51cm (20in) velvet braid
- 51cm (20in) pompom trimming
- 30cm (12in) strip fasteners of velcro

FOR THE HAIR AND FACE
- 1 ball wool (yellow)
- 10cm (4in) bias binding (yellow)
- 10cm (4in) narrow ribbon
- 11mm (⅜in) self-cover button
- Tailor's chalk
- Embroidery threads (red, black)
- Scraps felt (2 shades of blue)

CUTTING OUT
BODY: plump doll's pattern pieces, pages 44-7
SHOES: plump doll's pattern piece, page 53
CLOTHES: pattern pieces, pages 62-5

◆ BODY ◆
Make up the body following the instructions on page 7.

◆ SHOES ◆
Make up the shoes following the instructions on page 10.

◆ PANTALOONS ◆
1 Make up the pantaloons following the instructions on page 10.
2 Sew small ribbon roses around the elasticated hem of each leg.

◆ DRESS ◆
1 Machine stitch the dress front to the back pieces at the shoulders with a 5mm (¼in) seam. Press the seams flat.
2 Place the sleeves on the shoulders with the centre of the sleeve matching the centre seam of the shoulder and with the right sides facing. You might find it easier to baste the pieces together before machine stitching. Allow a 5mm (¼in) seam and press the seams open when finished.
3 On each cuff, turn over 1cm (⅜in) of fabric to the wrong side and machine stitch. Hand sew a piece of rick-rack braid around each cuff of the sleeve.
4 With right sides facing and starting at the end of each sleeve, sew up the side seam of the first sleeve and down the side of the dress allowing a 5mm (¼in) seam. Repeat on the other side. Press the seams open.
5 Cut out spots of fabric and stick or stitch them onto the dress.
6 Fold the neck seam over to neaten, press and then machine stitch a strip of rick-rack braid in place.
7 On each side at the back opening, turn over 2cm (¾in) to the wrong side, press and machine stitch. Trim the raw edges with pinking shears.
8 Sew a collection of braids and pompom trimming around the hem of the dress, stitching one braid over another.
9 To hold the dress closed, sew on a line of fasteners or a strip of velcro.

◆ HAIR ◆
1 Cut approximately 100 strands of wool for the main hair (this is only a guideline as it is up to you how thick and long you wish to make the hair). Lay the centre of the strands of wool evenly on a strip of similar-coloured bias binding and sew them down using either hand or machine stitch. If you have problems keeping the wool strands still while sewing you can always fasten them down with a dab of fabric glue.
2 For the fringe, cut approximately 50 strands to the same length as the main hair. Lay the strands of wool on another strip of bias binding. The bias binding should lie approximately 5cm (2in) from one end of the strands. Again secure the strands using hand or machine stitch.
3 To attach the hair to the doll's head, first sew down the fringe piece, with the strip of bias binding running over the top of the head from side to side. Do this using a similar coloured thread making suitably neat, small running stitches.
4 Then attach the main hair piece so that it runs at right angles to the other piece, forming a parting in the middle. Trim your doll's hair to the desired length.
5 Tie a ribbon bow and sew it on the front of the hair.

◆ FACE ◆
1 Cover the 11mm (⅜in) button with a piece of the face fabric and stitch onto the face, slightly below the centre.
2 Mark the shape of the mouth with a piece of tailor's chalk. Using red embroidery thread, stitch on the mouth.
3 Cut two small oval shapes out of dark blue felt and stick them onto the face using the fabric glue.
4 Cut two smaller circles out of a lighter blue felt and stick them onto the dark blue felt. Sew small black lines of embroidery thread to indicate eyelashes.

FATHER CHRISTMAS

Father Christmas is a cuddly favourite among all young children and is always remembered for his charm and generosity every year. To create an even cuddlier Father Christmas, I have used soft and fluffy mohair wool to make his beard. You can even make him a present sack and fill it with your own supply of tasty sweets and chocolates.

YOU WILL NEED
FOR THE BODY
- 31 x 100cm (12 x 39in) calico or cotton
- 18 x 40cm (7 x 16in) cotton jersey
- Scissors
- Dressmaker's pins
- Cotton threads (to match fabrics)
- Sewing machine
- Iron and ironing board
- Needle
- 250g (8oz) washable stuffing

FOR THE CLOTHES
- Fabrics (see patterns for quantity)
- Pinking shears
- 53 x 10cm (21 x 4in) felt (white)
- 81cm (32in) piece 5mm (¼in) wide elastic
- Safety pin
- 30cm (12in) strip fasteners or velcro
- 51cm (20in) ribbon (black)
- Brass buckle
- Pompom (white)

FOR THE HAIR, BEARD AND FACE
- 1 ball wool (white)
- 11mm (⅜in) self-cover button
- Tailor's chalk
- Embroidery thread (red)
- Scrap felt (black)
- Fabric glue

CUTTING OUT
BODY: plump doll's pattern pieces, pages 44-7
SHOES: plump doll's pattern piece, page 53
CLOTHES: pattern pieces, page 95; plus dress (coat) front, back and sleeves on pages 62-5 and trousers on pages 70-1

◆ BODY ◆
Make up the body following the instructions on page 7.

◆ SHOES ◆
Make up the shoes following the instructions on page 10.

◆ TROUSERS ◆
1 Follow the instructions for pantaloons Steps 1 and 2 on page 10.
2 At the bottom of the legs, turn up 1cm (⅜in) of fabric to make a hem and press. Sew a strip of white felt around each hem. Depending on how wide the strip is, sew one or two lines of stitching to keep it in place.
3 Follow pantaloons Step 4 on page 10.

◆ COAT AND BELT ◆
1 Reverse all markings given on the pattern pieces for this coat on pages 62-5 so that back becomes front, and front back. This coat is really the same dress pattern, but put on back to front. Machine stitch the coat back to the two front pieces at the shoulders, with a 5mm (¼in) seam. Press the seam open.
2 Place the sleeves on the shoulders with the centre of the sleeve matching the centre seam of the shoulder and with the right sides facing. You might find it easier to baste the pieces together before machine stitching. Allow a 5mm (¼in) seam and press the seams open when finished.
3 On each cuff of the sleeve, turn over 1cm (⅜in) of fabric to the wrong side, carefully press and machine stitch in place.
4 With right sides facing and starting at the end of each sleeve, sew up the side seam of the first sleeve and down the side of the coat allowing a 5mm (¼in) seam. Repeat on the other side. Press the seams open.
5 Press the neck seam over to neaten and machine stitch.
6 On each side at the front opening, turn over 2cm (¾in) to the wrong side and machine stitch. Trim the raw edges with pinking shears.
7 Cut two strips of white felt the same width and sew one down the outside centre front of the coat and the other around the hem.
8 To hold the coat closed, sew on a line of fasteners or a strip of velcro.

9 For the belt, cut a piece of the ribbon to fit around the waist and thread it through the buckle. To fasten the belt around the body, sew on a fastener or a small piece of velcro.

◆ HAIR AND BEARD ◆
1 Make 15 bundles of wool, each comprising approximately ten strands of wool. Tie a length of wool around the centre of each pile and knot firmly.
2 Sew the knots onto the face and head to make a large beard and a short hair style. Trim to neaten.

◆ HAT ◆
1 Sew the two pieces of fabric together along the straight seam and turn right sides out.
2 Sew a strip of white felt around the rim of the hat and sew a pompom onto the point of the hat. Then sew the hat onto the head with small, neat stitches for security.

◆ FACE ◆
1 Cover the 11mm (⅜in) button with a piece of the face fabric and stitch onto the face, slightly below the centre.
2 Mark the shape of the mouth with a piece of tailor's chalk. Using red embroidery thread, stitch on the mouth.
3 For the eyes, cut two small circles out of the black felt and stick them onto the face.

◆ BAG ◆
1 With right sides facing, machine stitch along the bottom and side seams.
2 Turn the top edge of the bag over 2.5cm (1in) onto the wrong side of the fabric. Machine stitch 2cm (¾in) down from the fold, all around the bag.
3 Thread a piece of black ribbon through the casing at the top and tie the two ends together in a knot to secure. Fill the bag with chocolates and sweets.

PLUMP DOLL'S BODY

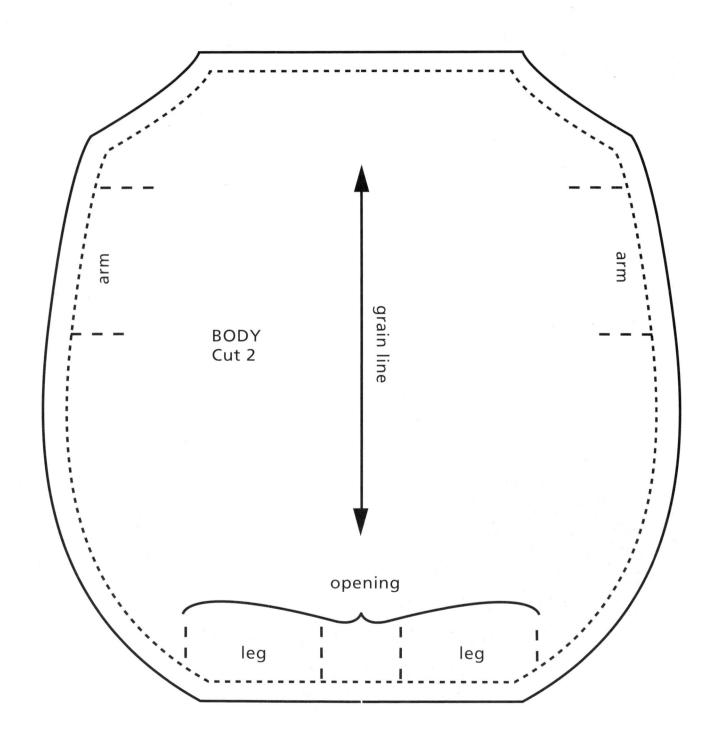

arm

arm

grain line

BODY
Cut 2

opening

leg

leg

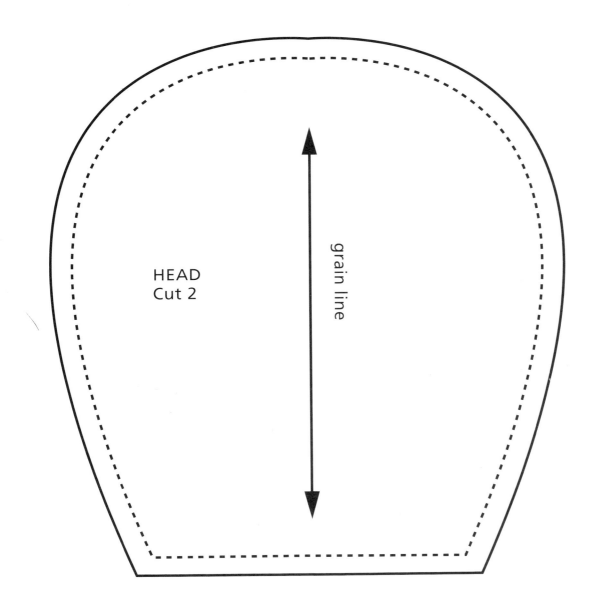

HEAD
Cut 2

grain line

pattern pieces continued overleaf

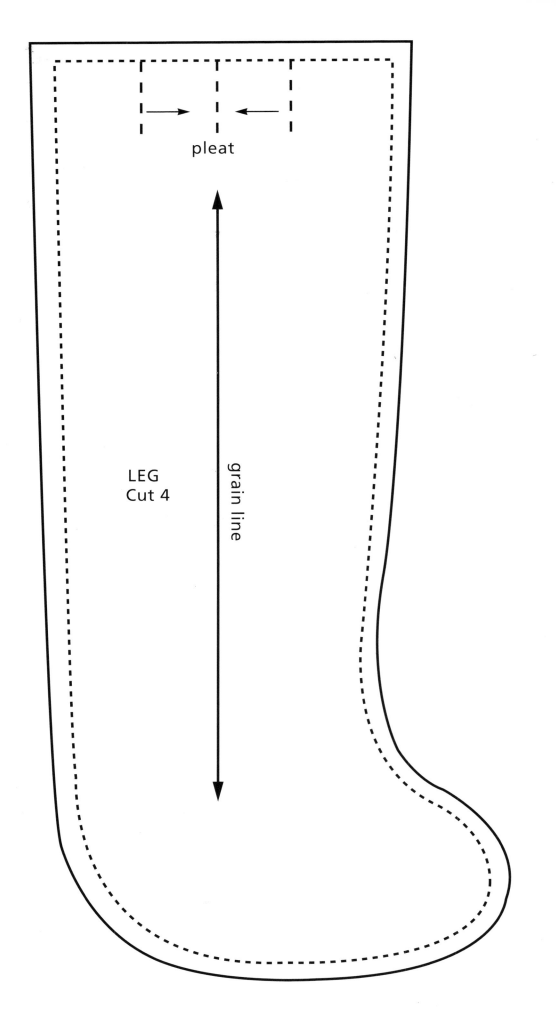

pleat

LEG
Cut 4

grain line

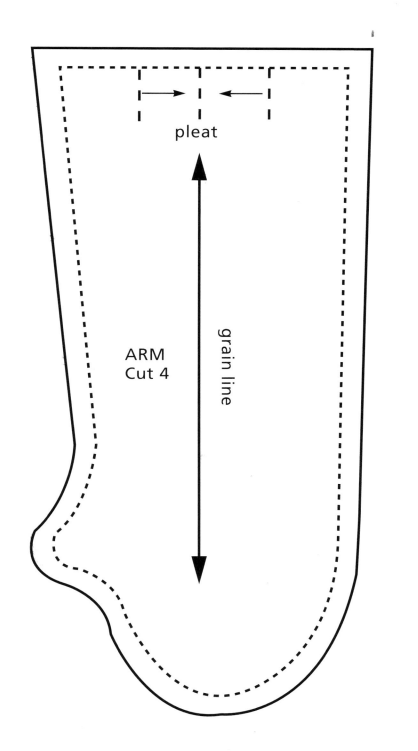

pleat

ARM
Cut 4

grain line

THIN DOLL'S BODY

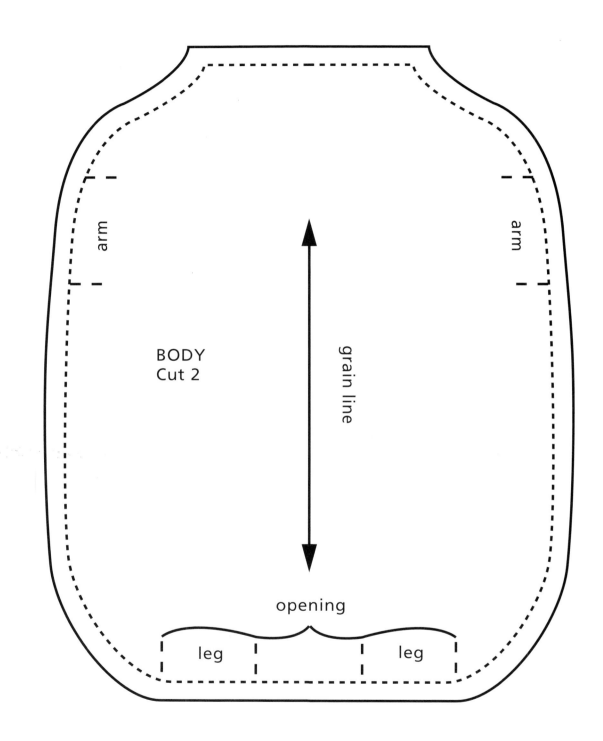

arm

arm

BODY
Cut 2

grain line

opening

leg

leg

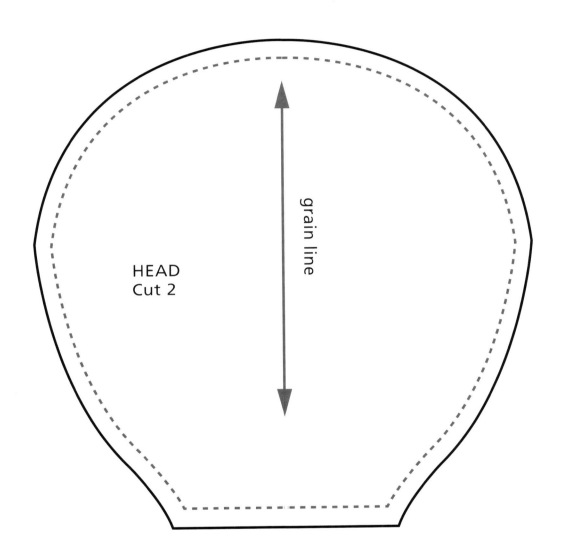

HEAD
Cut 2

grain line

pattern pieces continued overleaf

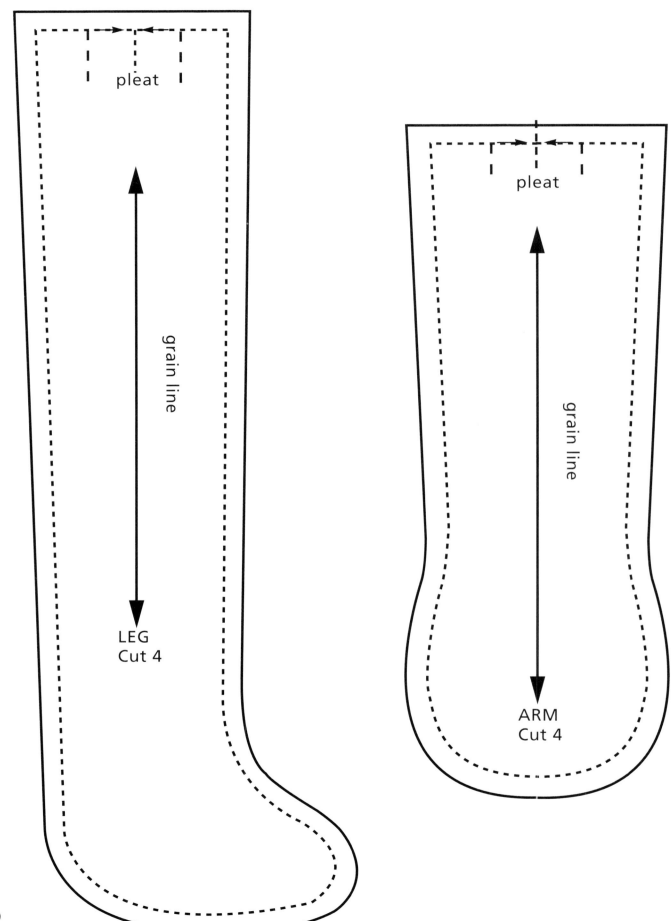

pleat

grain line

LEG
Cut 4

pleat

grain line

ARM
Cut 4

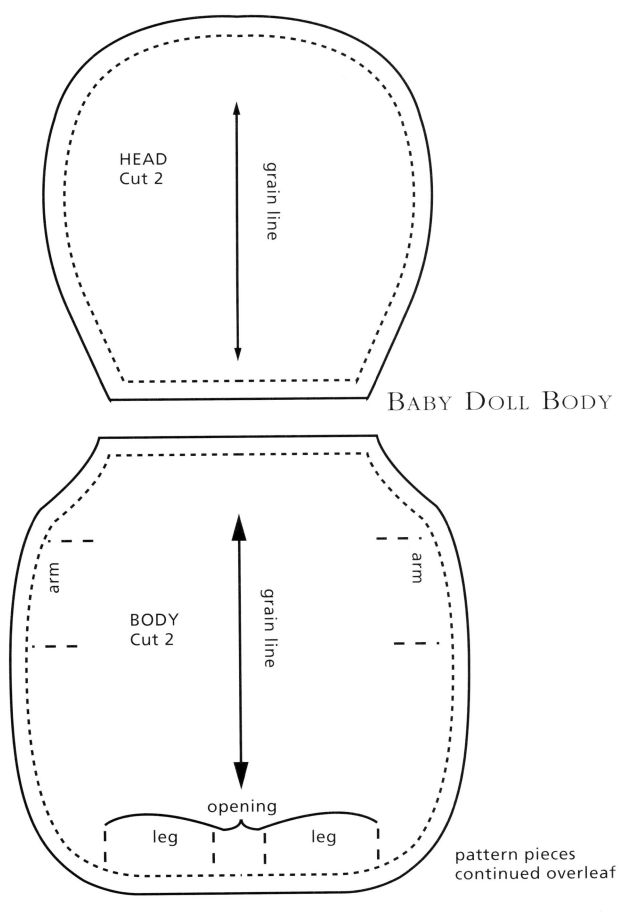

HEAD
Cut 2

grain line

BABY DOLL BODY

arm

arm

BODY
Cut 2

grain line

opening

leg

leg

pattern pieces
continued overleaf

51

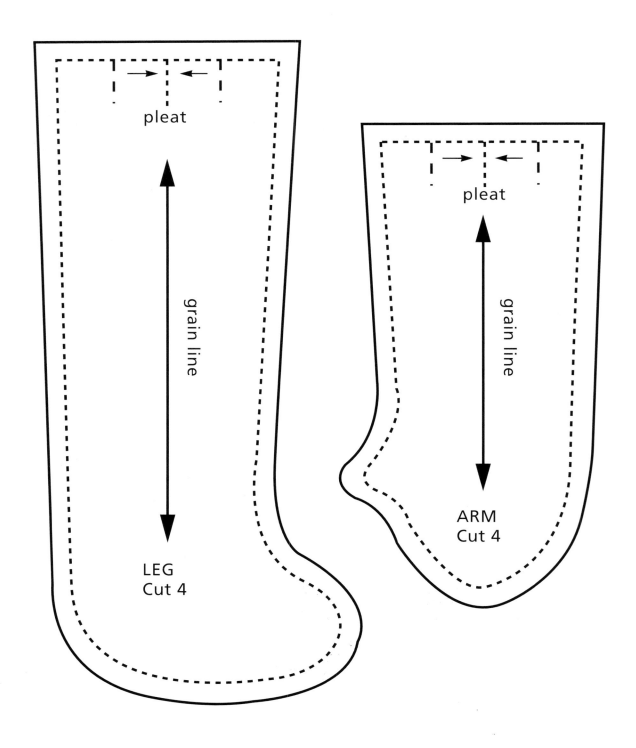

pleat

pleat

grain line

grain line

LEG
Cut 4

ARM
Cut 4

SHOES

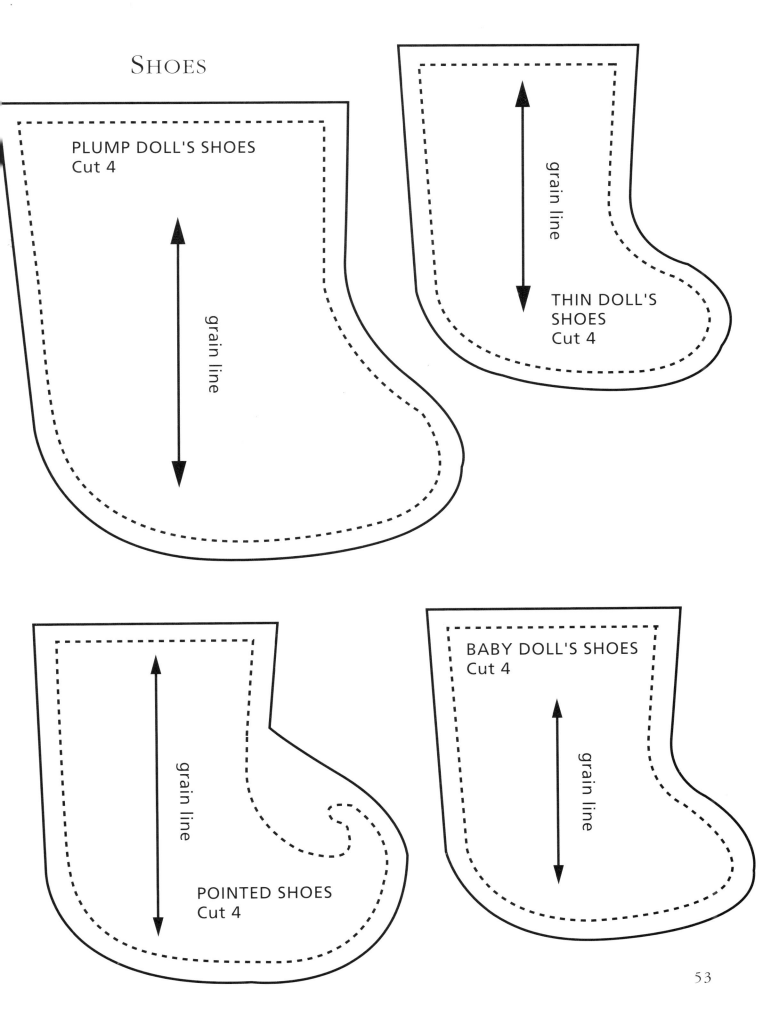

PLUMP DOLL'S SHOES
Cut 4

grain line

THIN DOLL'S
SHOES
Cut 4

grain line

POINTED SHOES
Cut 4

grain line

BABY DOLL'S SHOES
Cut 4

grain line

53

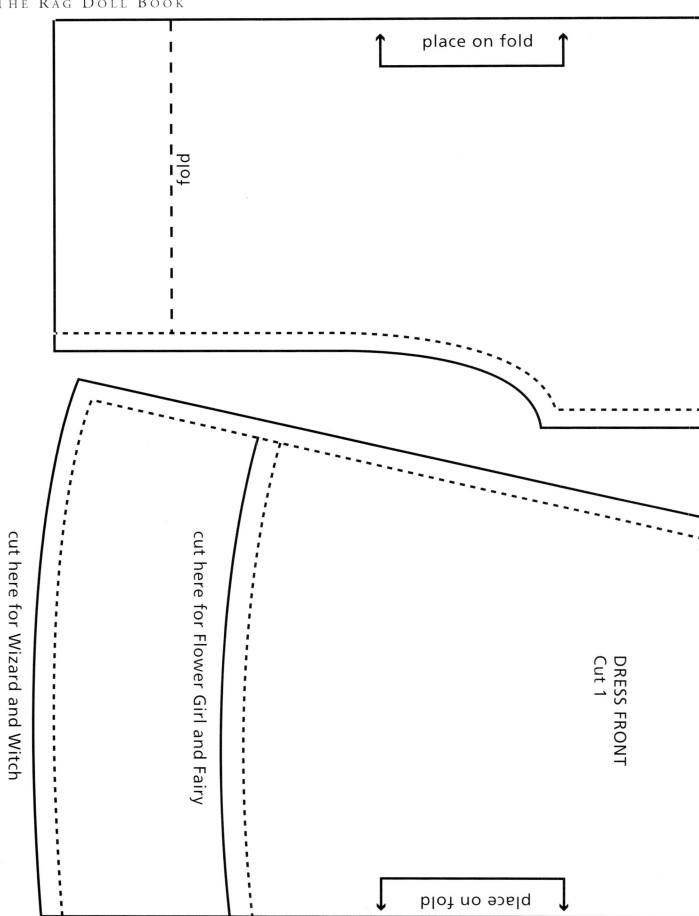

place on fold

fold

cut here for Wizard and Witch

cut here for Flower Girl and Fairy

DRESS FRONT
Cut 1

place on fold

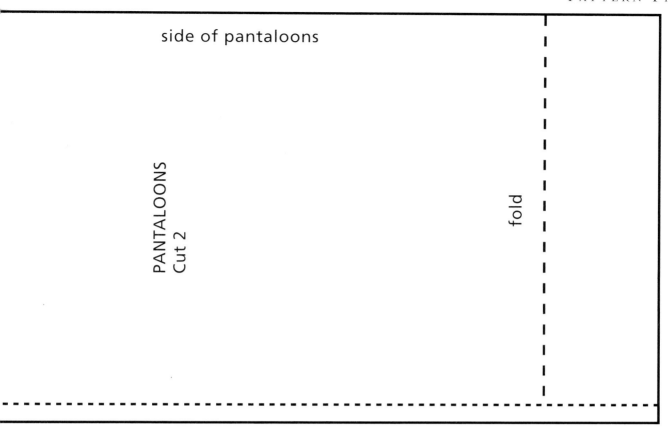

side of pantaloons

PANTALOONS
Cut 2

fold

FLOWER GIRL
(see page 10 for making instructions)

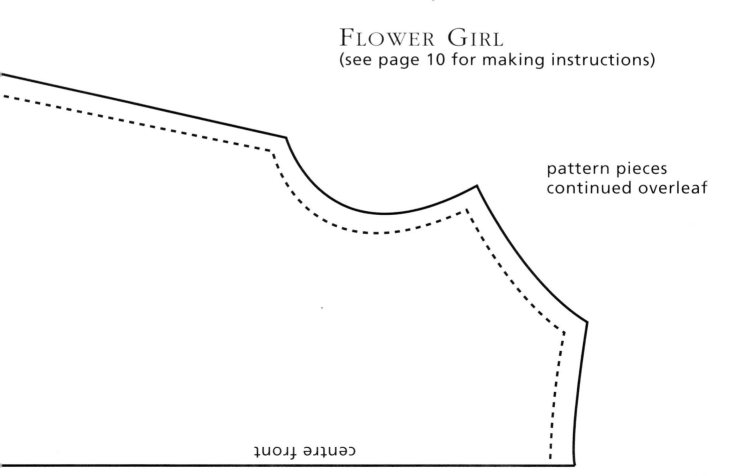

pattern pieces
continued overleaf

centre front

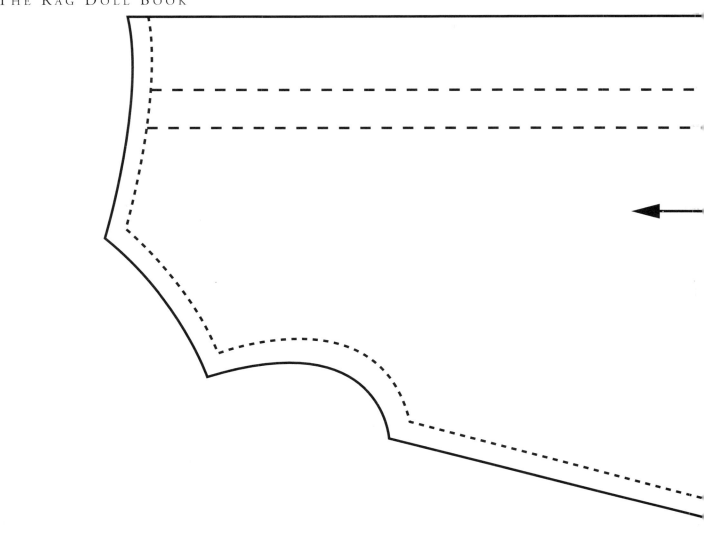

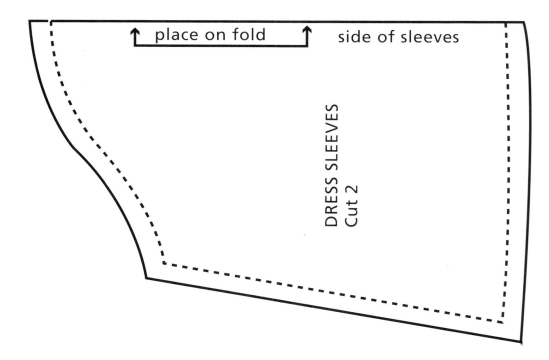

place on fold   side of sleeves

DRESS SLEEVES
Cut 2

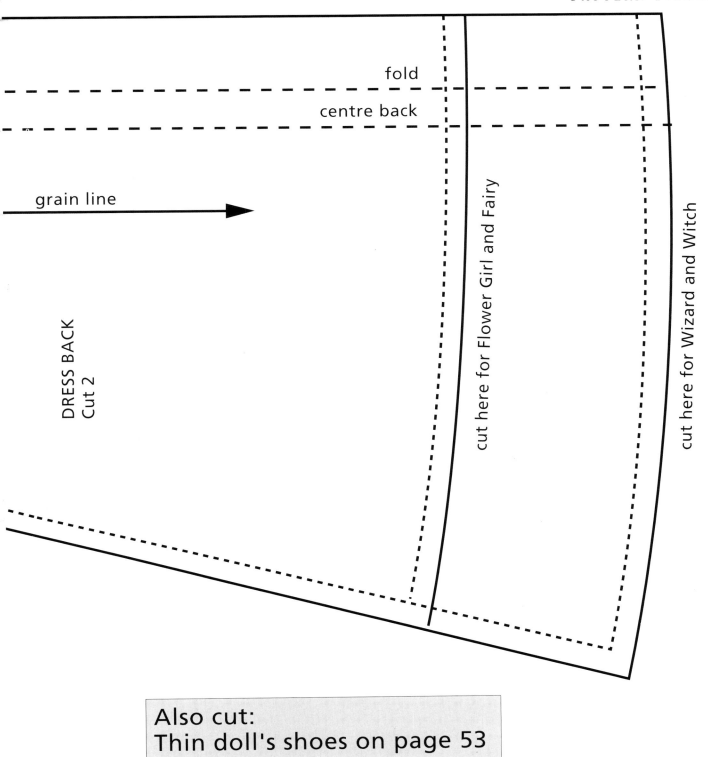

fold

centre back

grain line

DRESS BACK
Cut 2

cut here for Flower Girl and Fairy

cut here for Wizard and Witch

Also cut:
Thin doll's shoes on page 53

Shaker Boy
(see page 12 for making instructions)

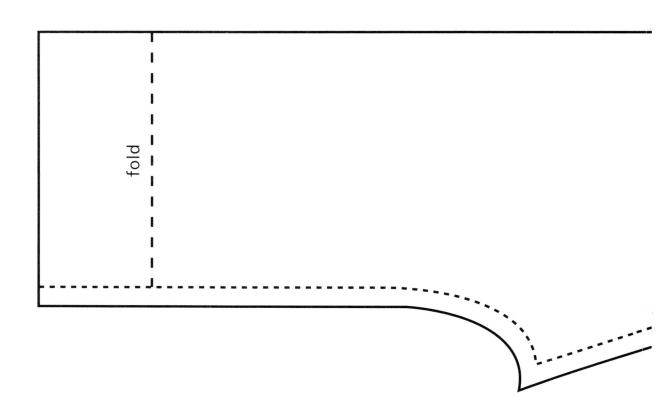

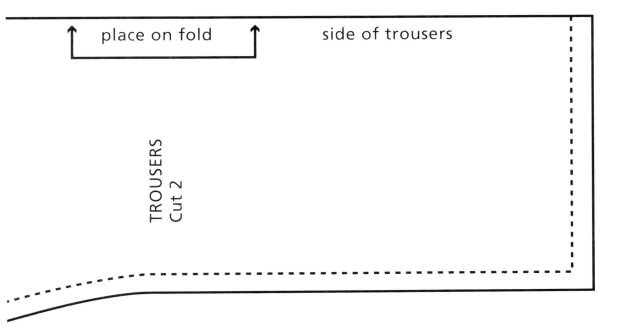

place on fold

side of trousers

TROUSERS
Cut 2

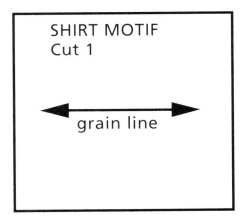

SHIRT MOTIF
Cut 1

grain line

grain line

SHIRT MOTIF
Cut 1

pattern pieces continued overleaf

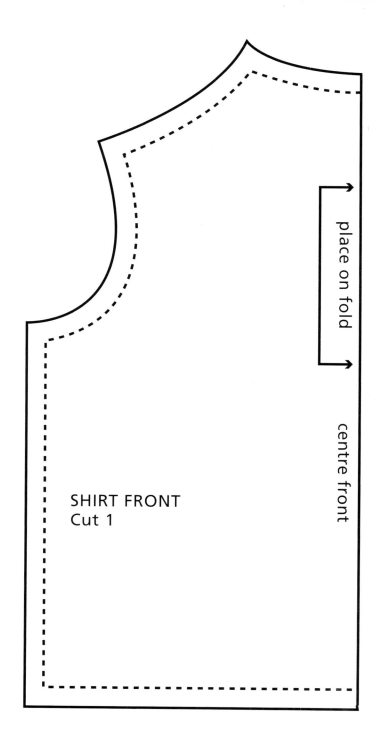

place on fold

centre front

SHIRT FRONT
Cut 1

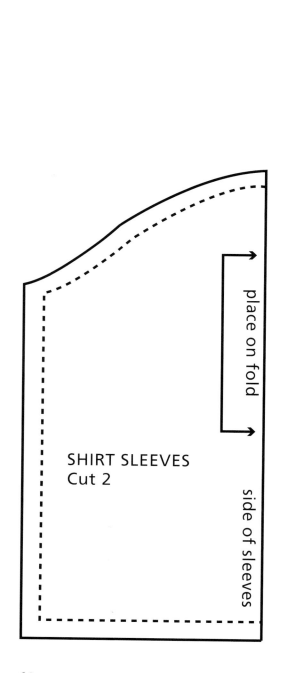

place on fold

side of sleeves

SHIRT SLEEVES
Cut 2

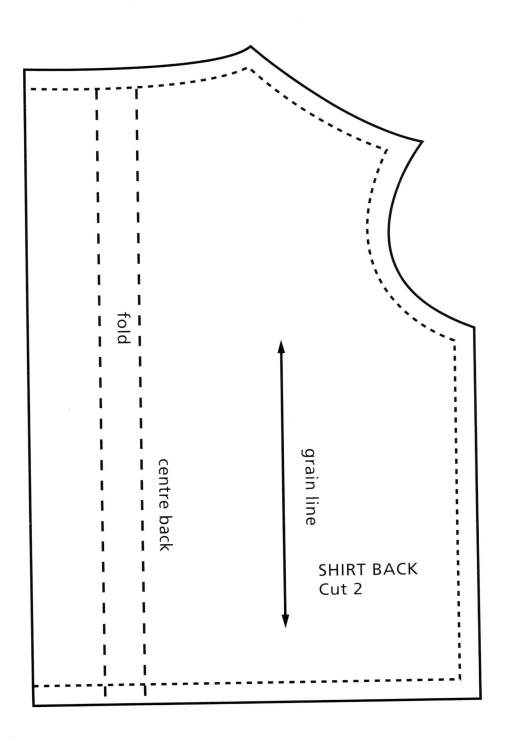

fold

centre back

grain line

SHIRT BACK
Cut 2

Also cut:
Thin doll's shoes on page 53

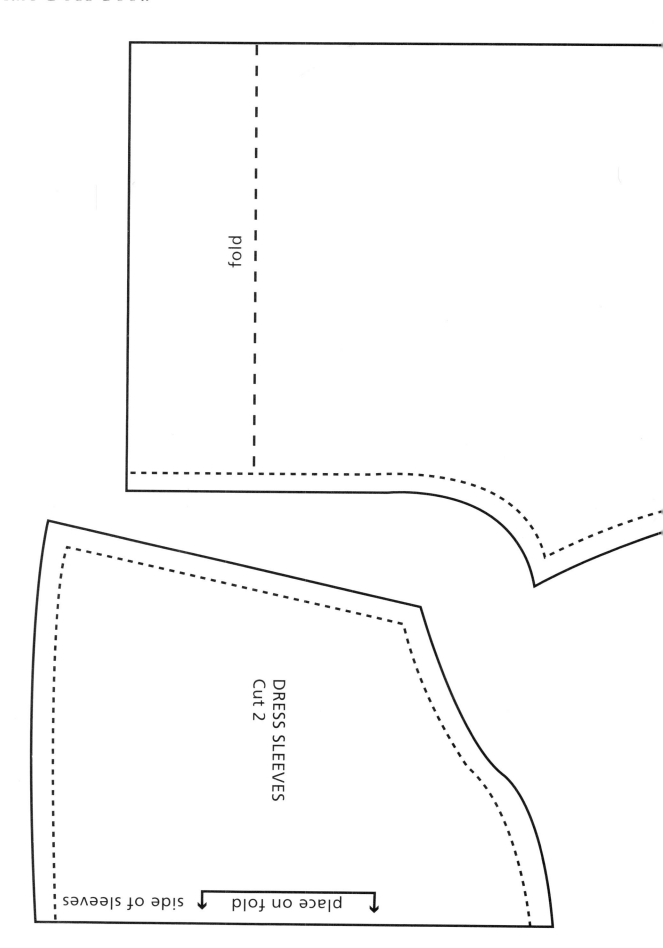

fold

DRESS SLEEVES
Cut 2

side of sleeves ↓ place on fold ↓

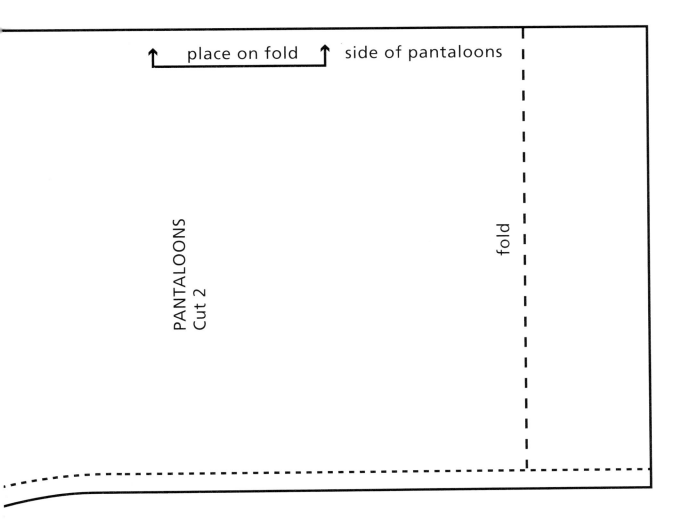

place on fold   side of pantaloons

PANTALOONS
Cut 2

fold

SHAKER GIRL, PARTY GIRLS (BIG SISTER) AND CIRCUS GIRL (see pages 14, 18 and 40 for making instructions)

pattern pieces continued overleaf

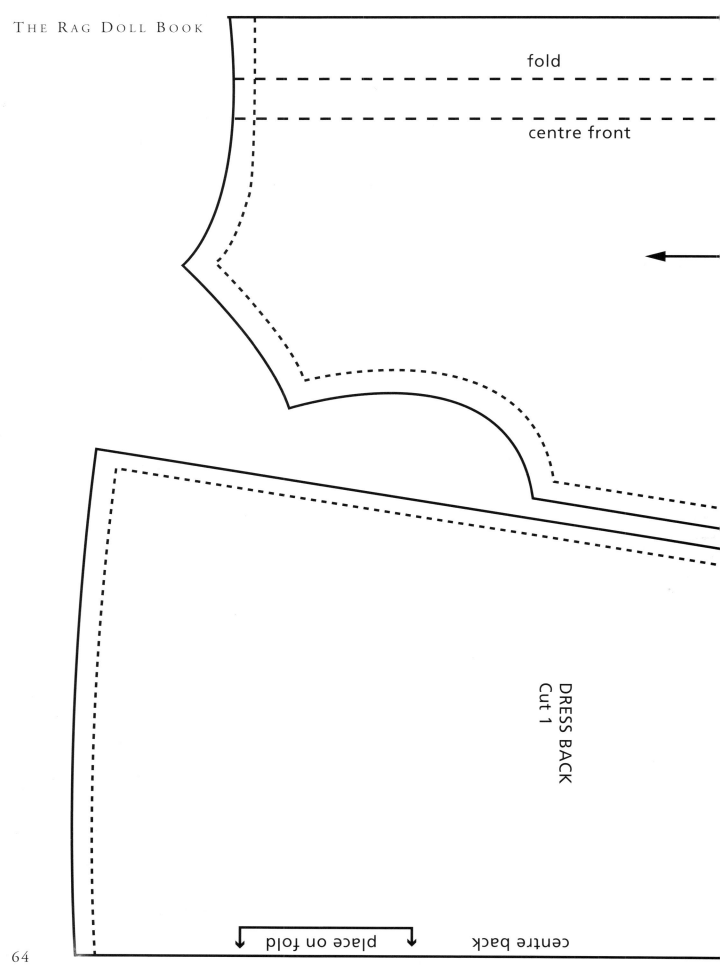

fold

centre front

DRESS BACK
Cut 1

centre back   place on fold

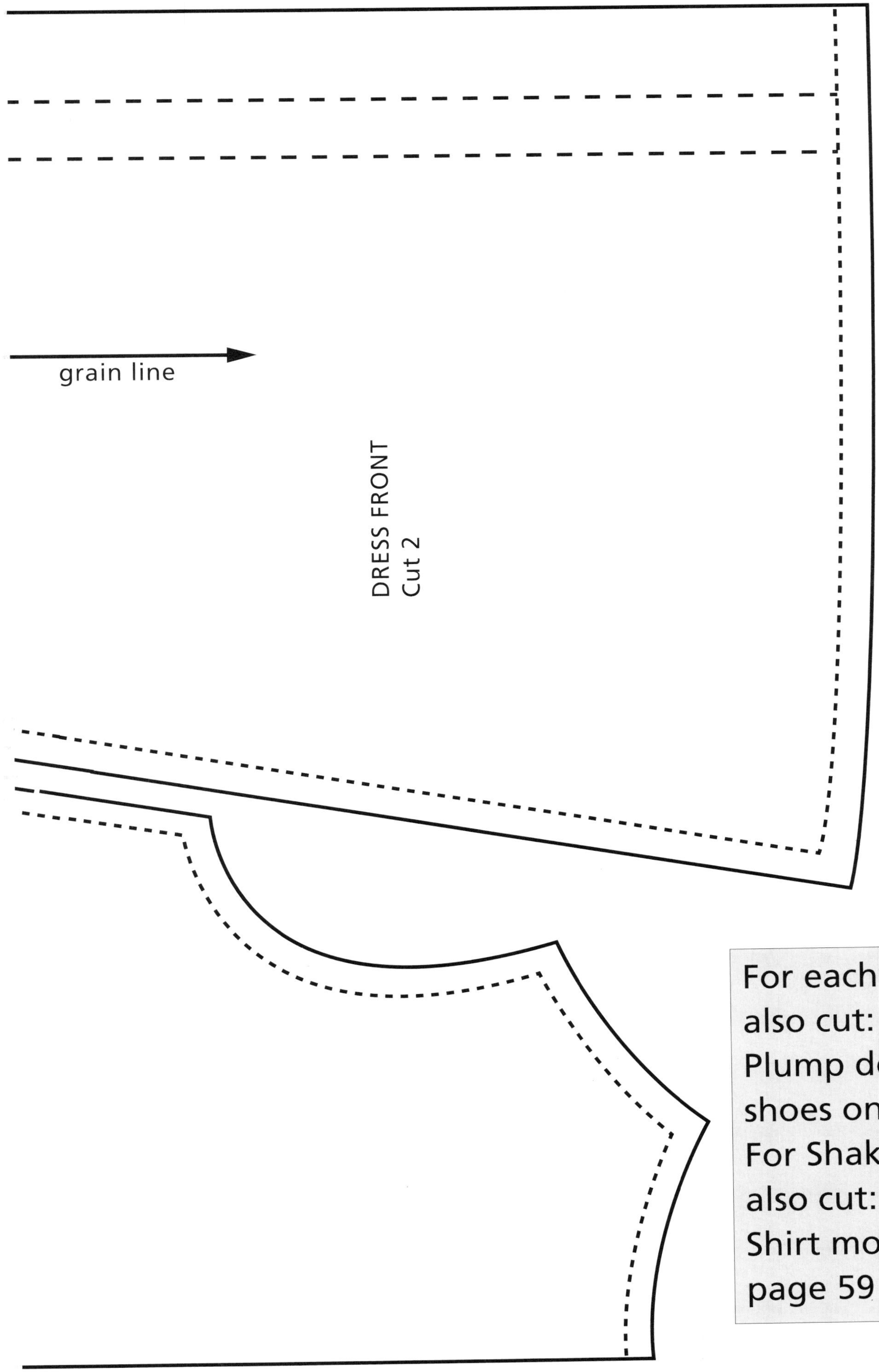

grain line

DRESS FRONT
Cut 2

For each doll,
also cut:
Plump doll's
shoes on page 53
For Shaker Girl,
also cut:
Shirt motifs on
page 59

PARLOUR MAID
(see page 16 for making
instructions)

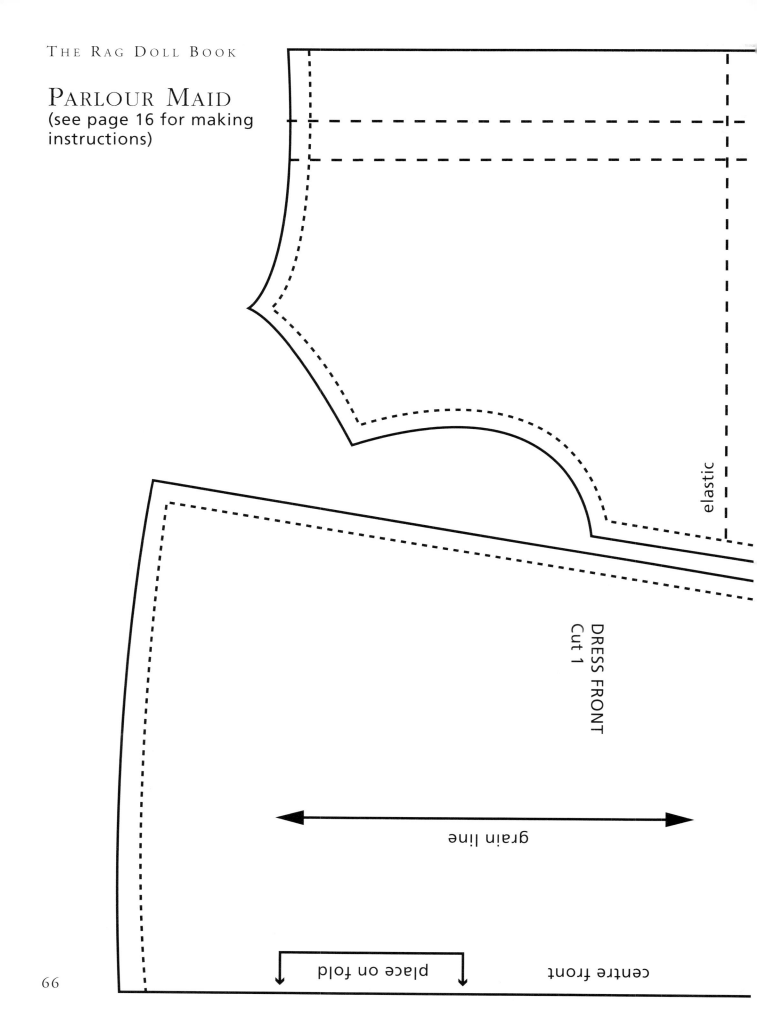

elastic

DRESS FRONT
Cut 1

grain line

place on fold

centre front

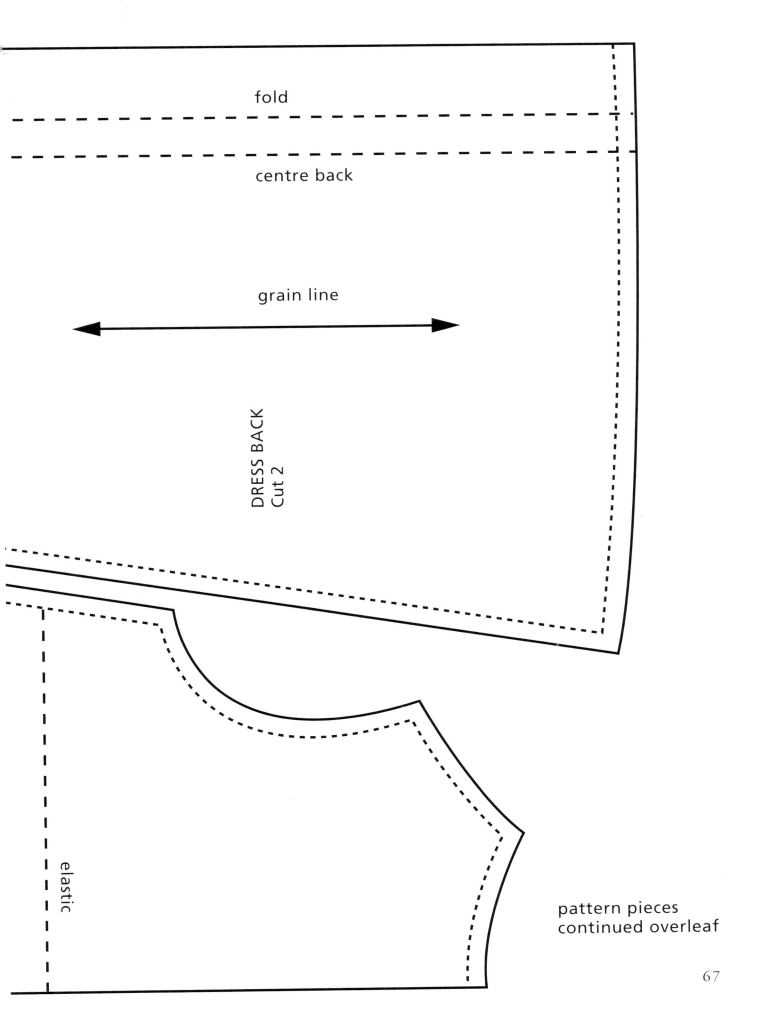

fold

centre back

grain line

DRESS BACK
Cut 2

elastic

pattern pieces
continued overleaf

67

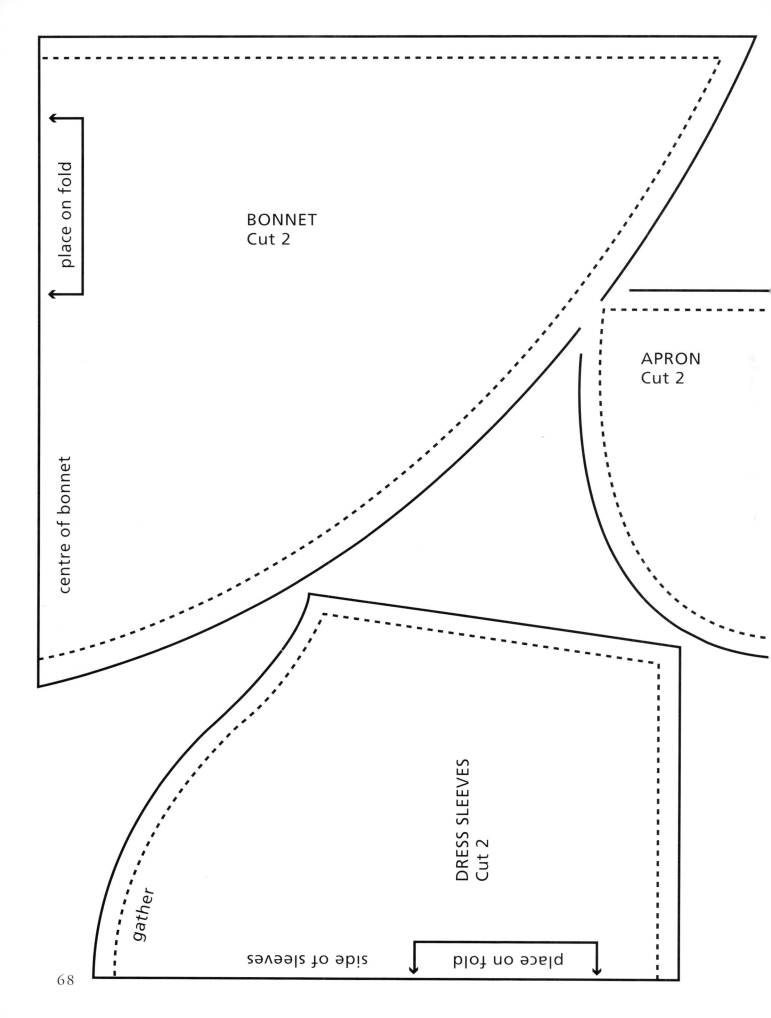

BONNET
Cut 2

place on fold

centre of bonnet

APRON
Cut 2

DRESS SLEEVES
Cut 2

gather

side of sleeves

place on fold

68

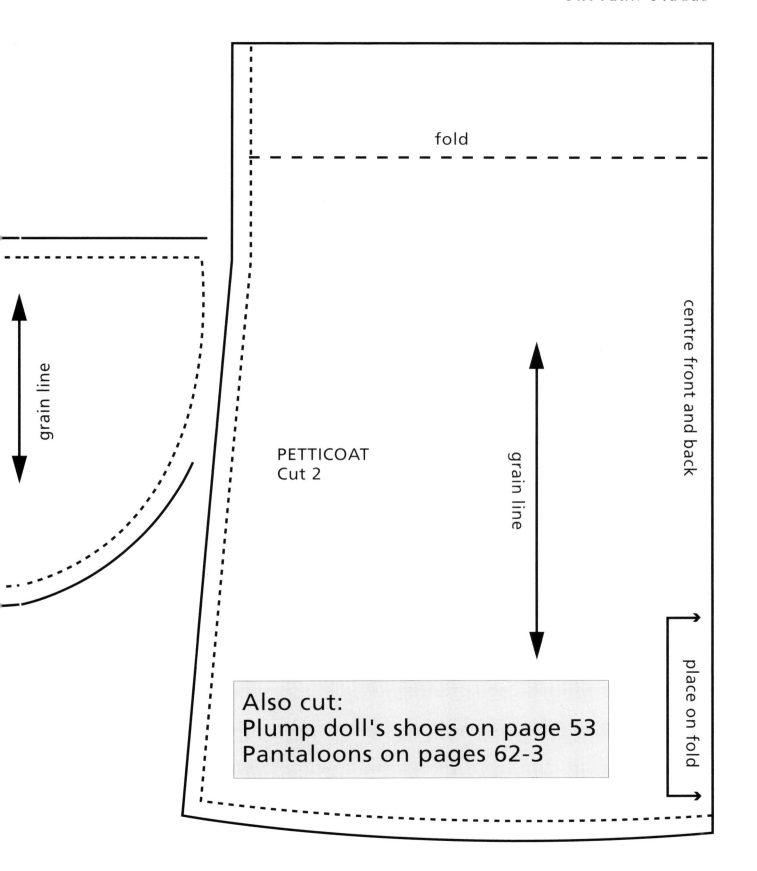

fold

centre front and back

grain line

PETTICOAT
Cut 2

grain line

place on fold

Also cut:
Plump doll's shoes on page 53
Pantaloons on pages 62-3

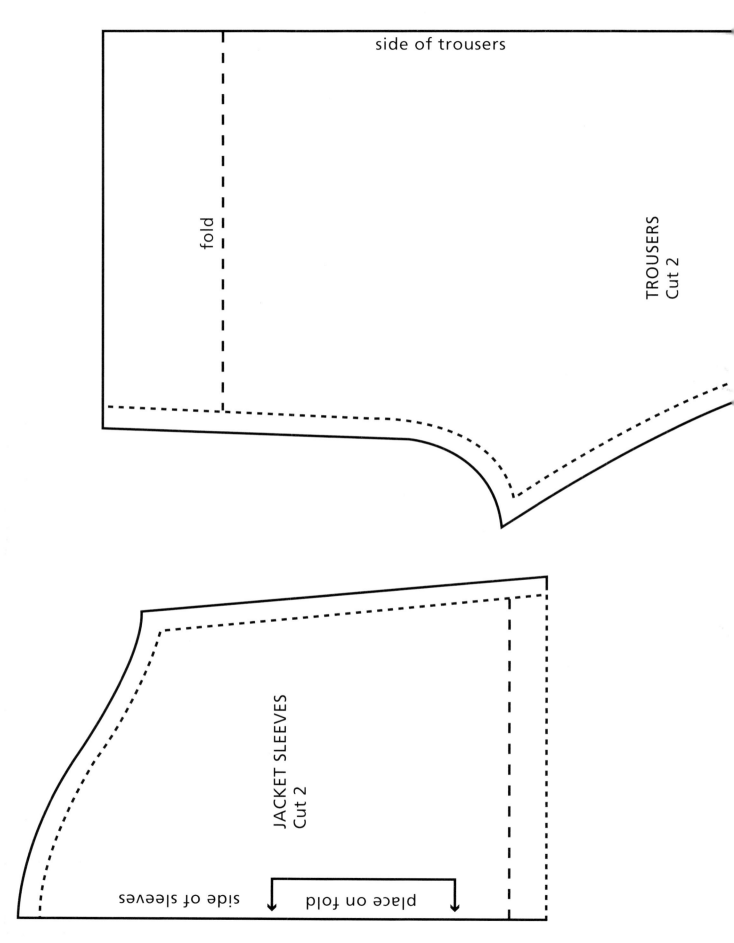

side of trousers

fold

TROUSERS
Cut 2

JACKET SLEEVES
Cut 2

side of sleeves

place on fold

place on fold

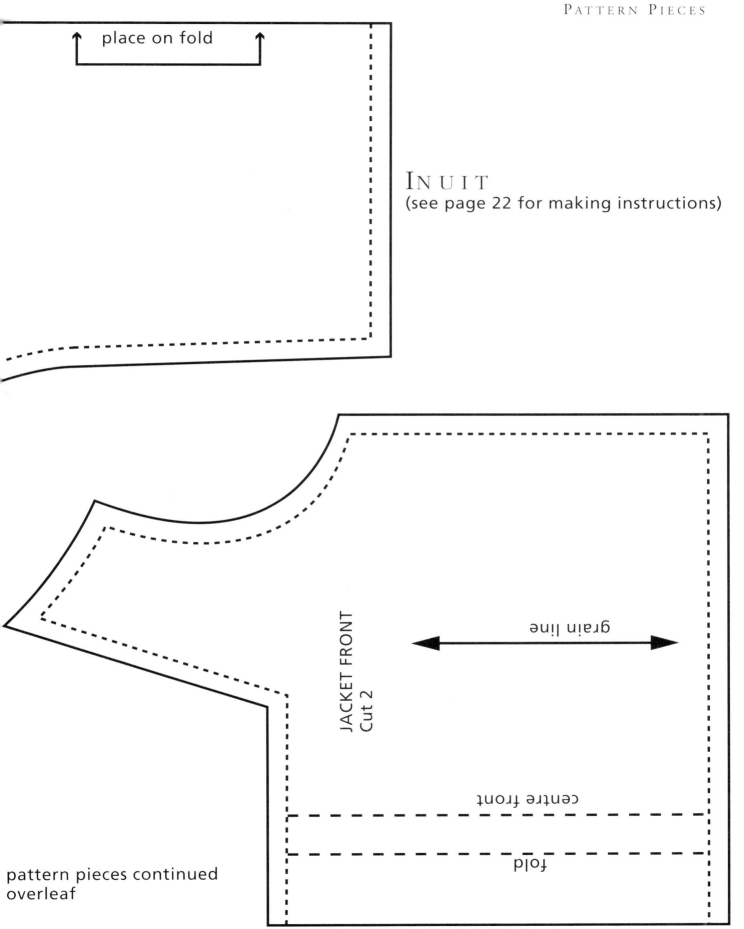

INUIT
(see page 22 for making instructions)

JACKET FRONT
Cut 2

grain line

centre front

fold

pattern pieces continued
overleaf

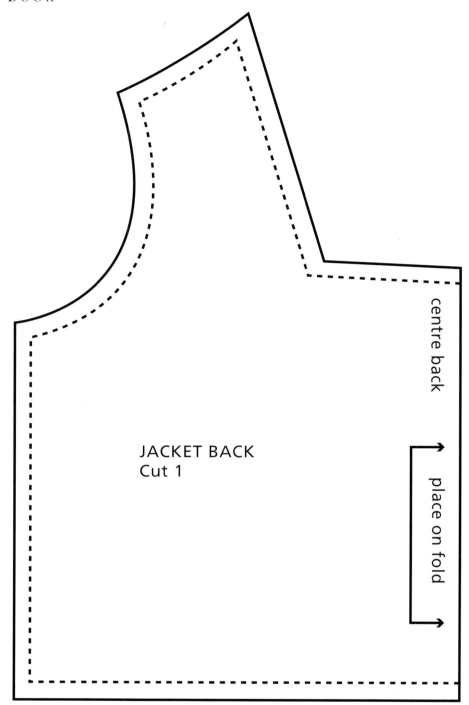

JACKET BACK
Cut 1

centre back

place on fold

Also cut:
Plump doll's shoes on page 53

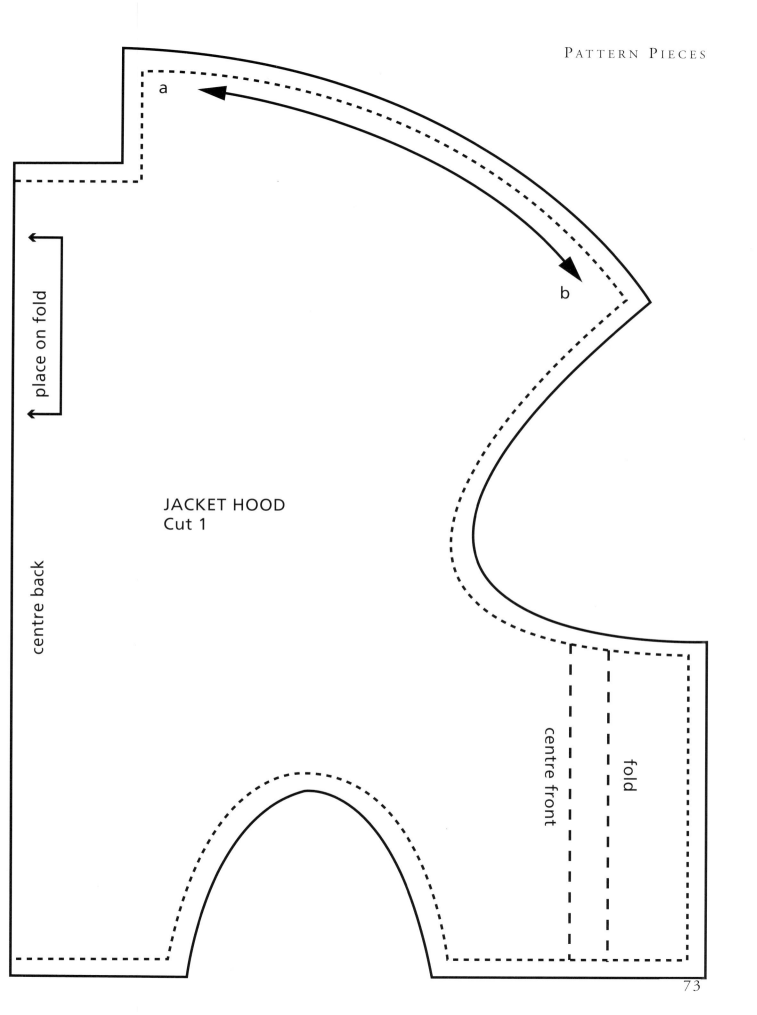

a

b

place on fold

centre back

JACKET HOOD
Cut 1

centre front

fold

Party Girls, Little Sister
(see page 20 for making instructions)

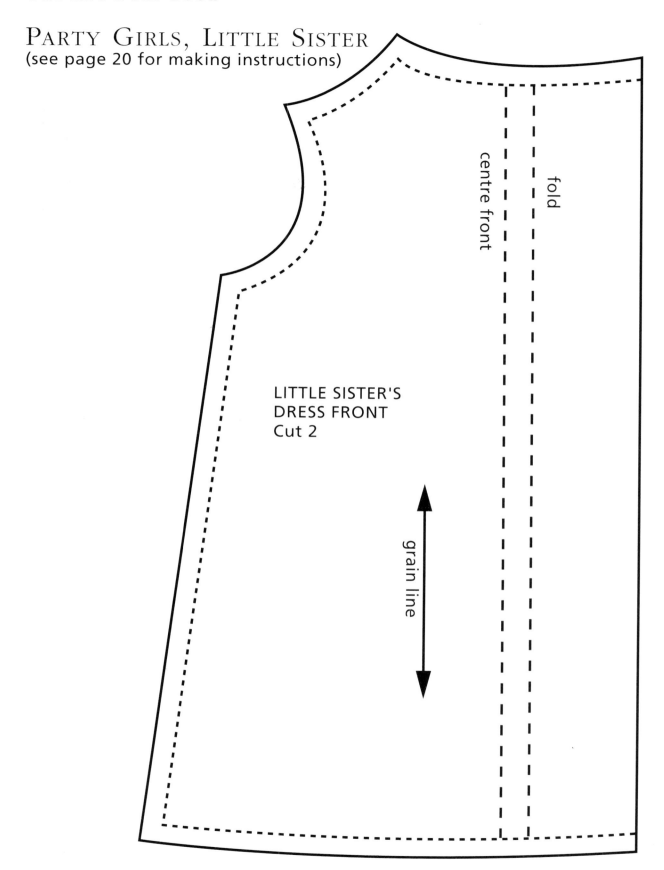

centre front

fold

LITTLE SISTER'S
DRESS FRONT
Cut 2

grain line

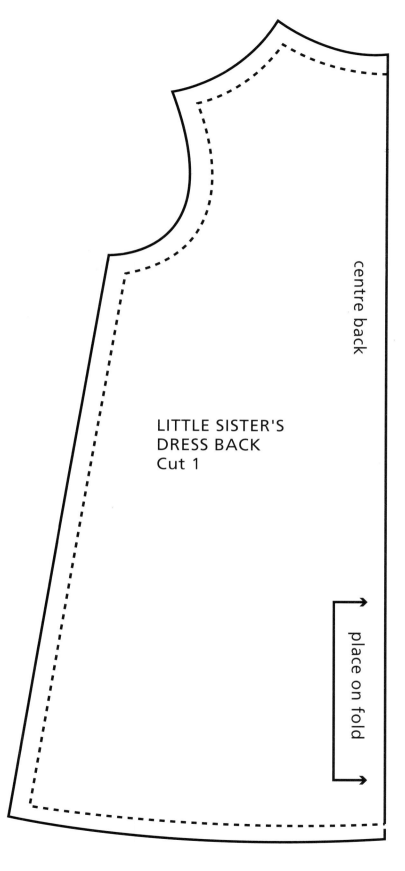

centre back

LITTLE SISTER'S
DRESS BACK
Cut 1

place on fold

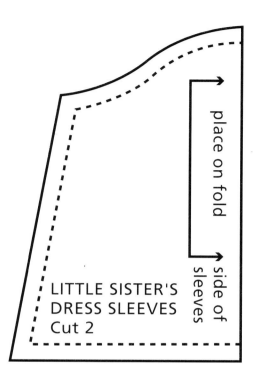

place on fold

side of sleeves

LITTLE SISTER'S
DRESS SLEEVES
Cut 2

pattern pieces continued overleaf

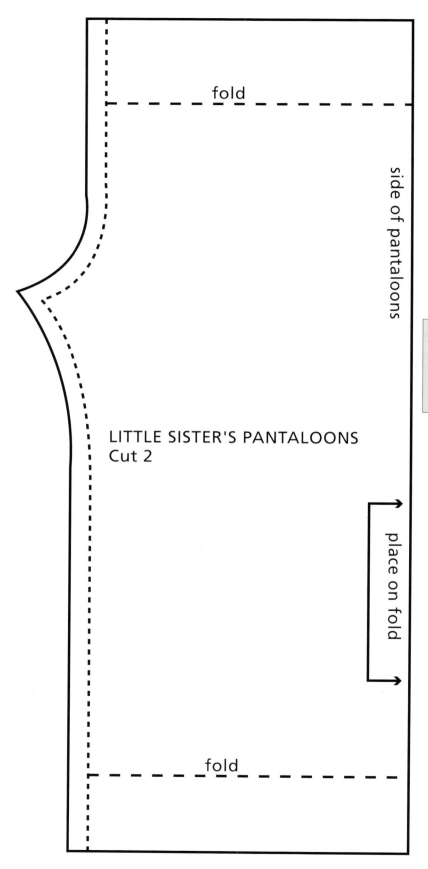

fold

side of pantaloons

LITTLE SISTER'S PANTALOONS
Cut 2

place on fold

fold

Also cut:
Baby doll's shoes on
page 53

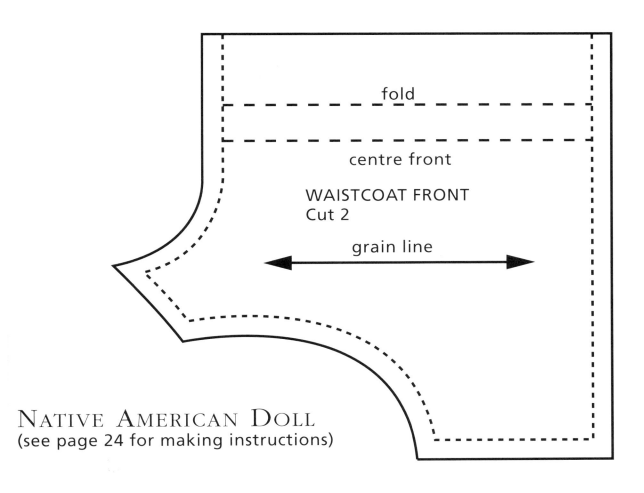

fold

centre front

WAISTCOAT FRONT
Cut 2

grain line

NATIVE AMERICAN DOLL
(see page 24 for making instructions)

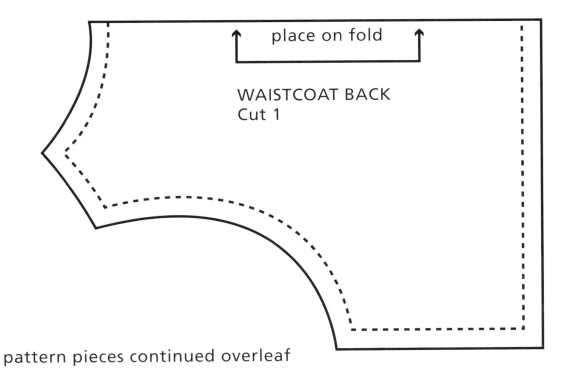

place on fold

WAISTCOAT BACK
Cut 1

pattern pieces continued overleaf

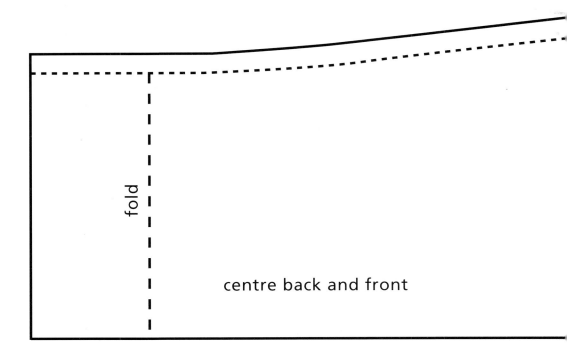

fold

centre back and front

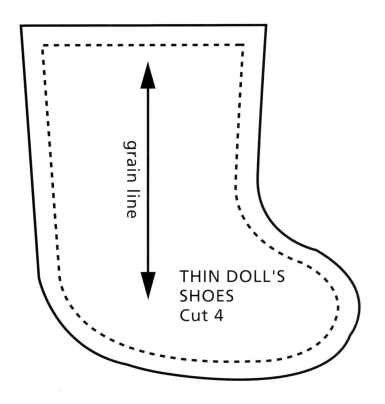

grain line

THIN DOLL'S
SHOES
Cut 4

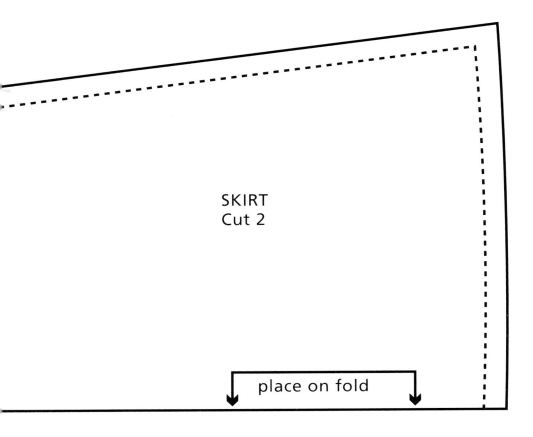

SKIRT
Cut 2

place on fold

Also cut:
Pantaloons on pages 54-5
Shirt front, back and sleeves on pages 60-1

Central American Doll
(see page 26 for making instructions)

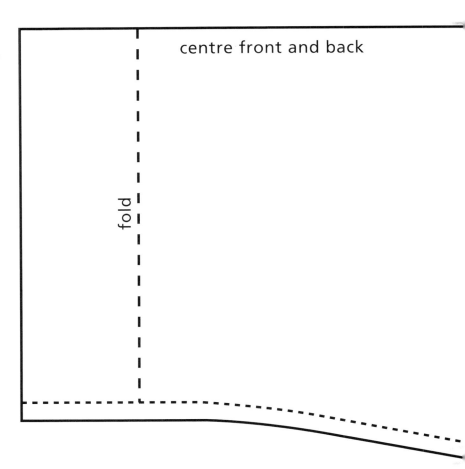

centre front and back

fold

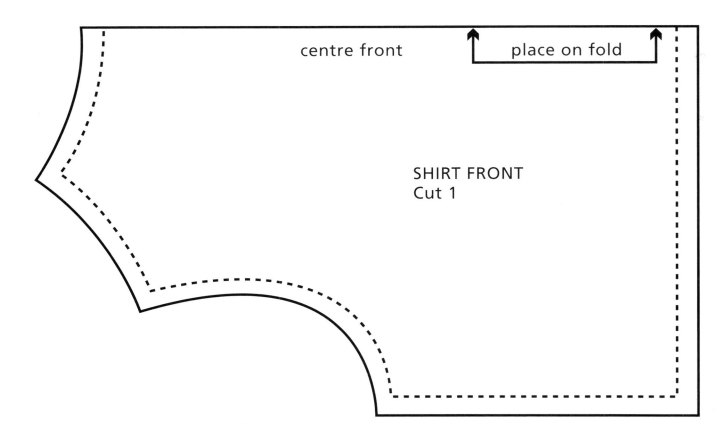

centre front   place on fold

SHIRT FRONT
Cut 1

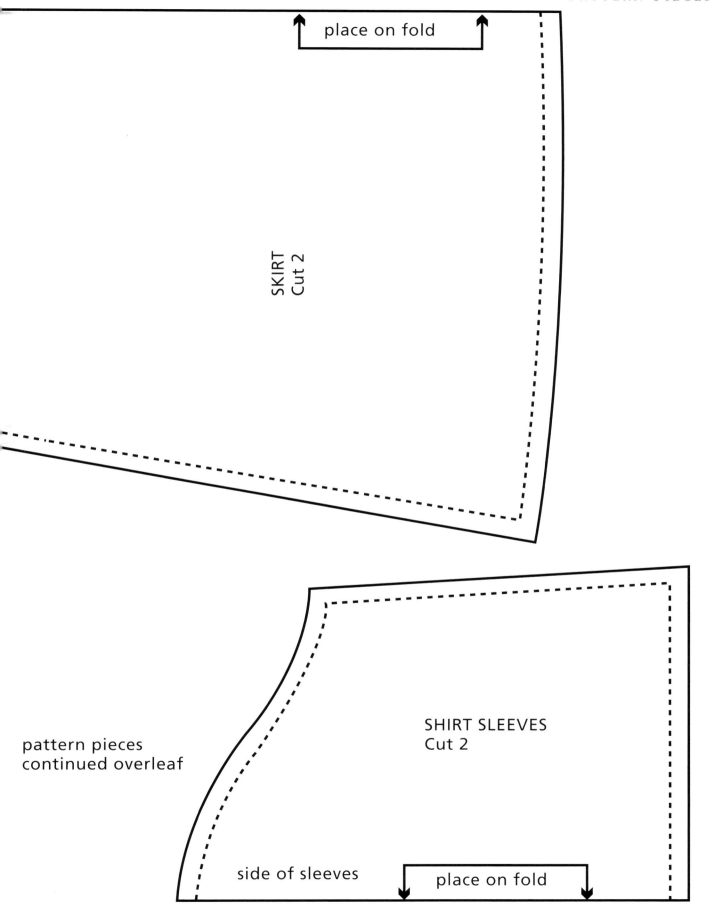

place on fold

SKIRT
Cut 2

pattern pieces
continued overleaf

SHIRT SLEEVES
Cut 2

side of sleeves

place on fold

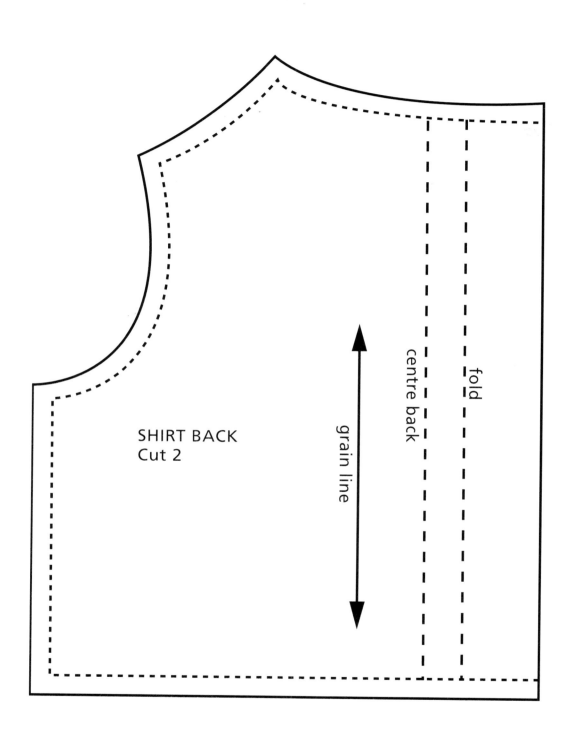

SHIRT BACK
Cut 2

grain line

centre back

fold

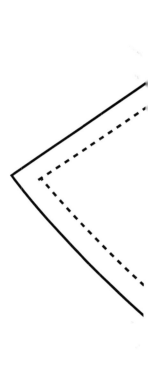

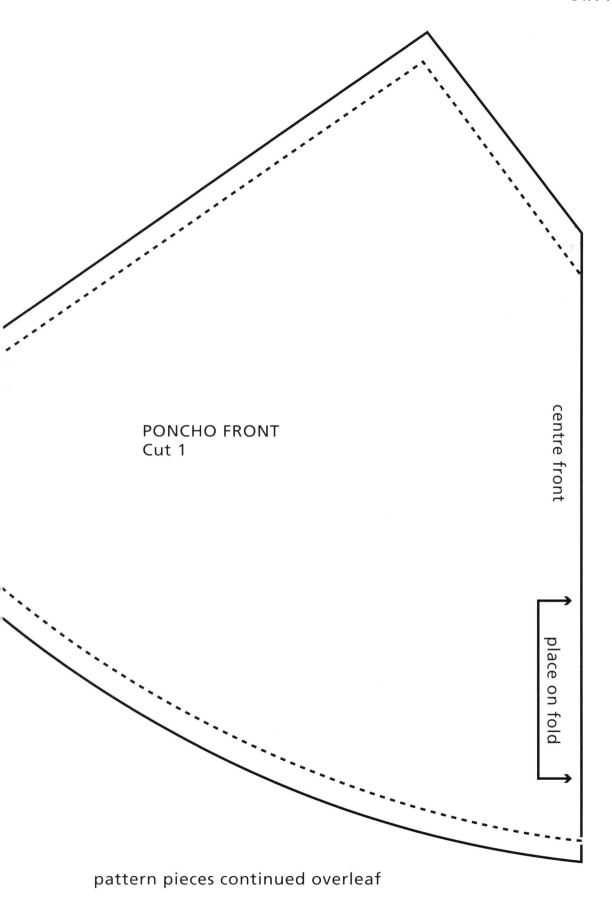

PONCHO FRONT
Cut 1

centre front

place on fold

pattern pieces continued overleaf

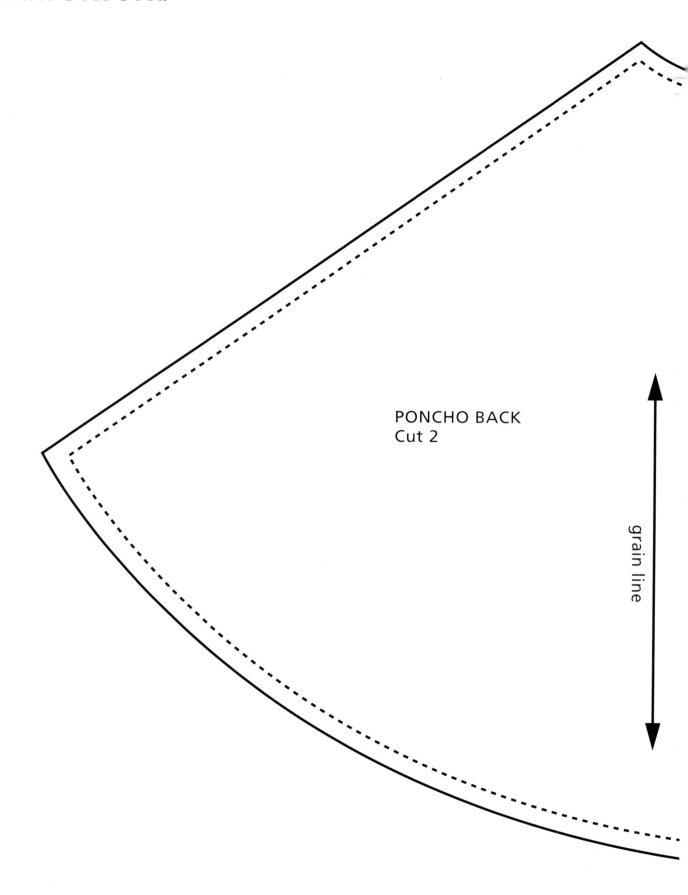

PONCHO BACK
Cut 2

grain line

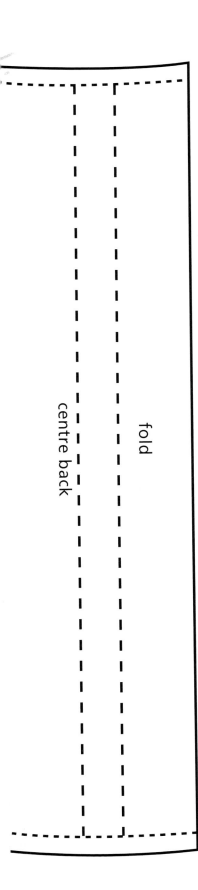

centre back

fold

Also cut:
Plump doll's shoes on page 53
Pantaloons on pages 62-3

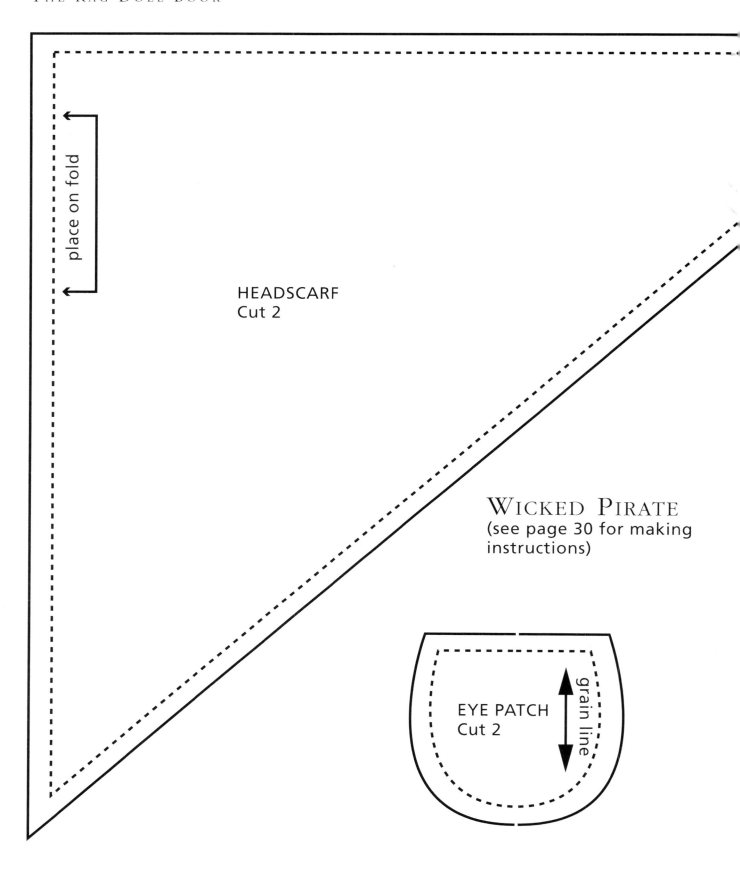

place on fold

HEADSCARF
Cut 2

WICKED PIRATE
(see page 30 for making
instructions)

EYE PATCH
Cut 2

grain line

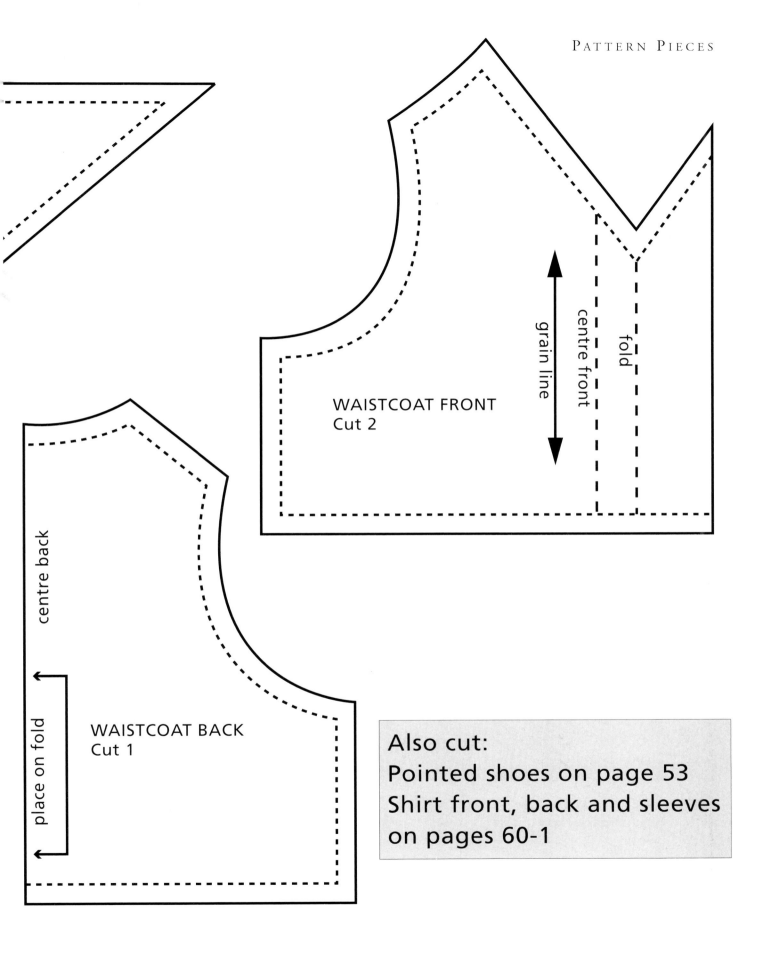

WAISTCOAT FRONT
Cut 2

grain line

centre front

fold

centre back

place on fold

WAISTCOAT BACK
Cut 1

Also cut:
Pointed shoes on page 53
Shirt front, back and sleeves
on pages 60-1

Fairy
(see page 32 for making instructions)

WING AND WAND STAR
Cut 2 in fabric
Cut 2 in silver card

Also cut
Thin doll's shoes on page 53
Pantaloons on pages 54-5
Dress front, back and sleeves on pages 54-7

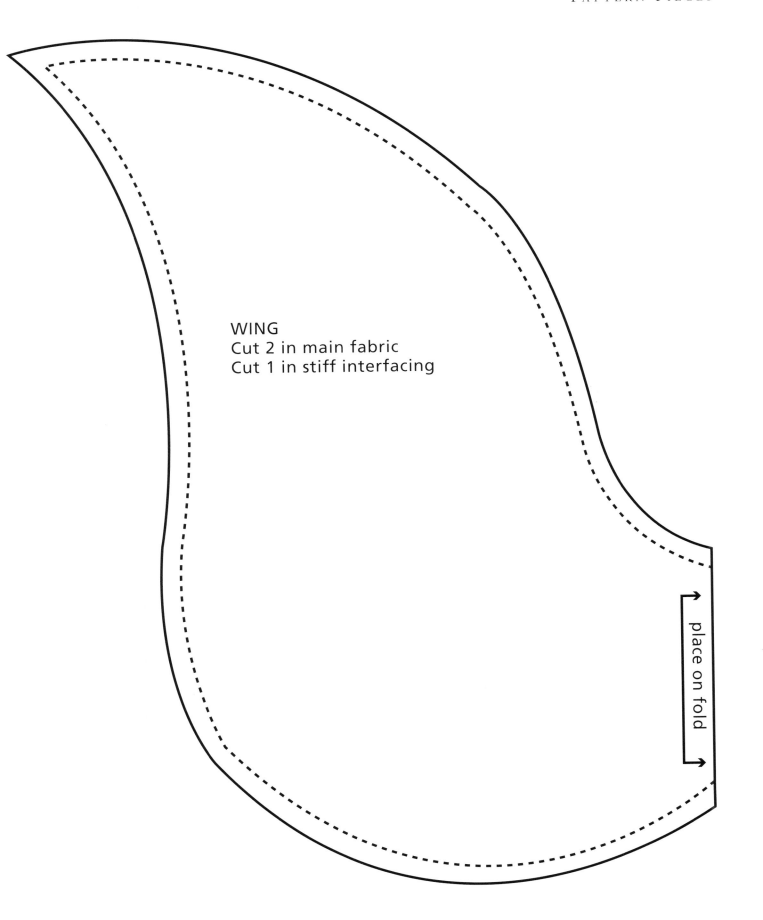

WING
Cut 2 in main fabric
Cut 1 in stiff interfacing

place on fold

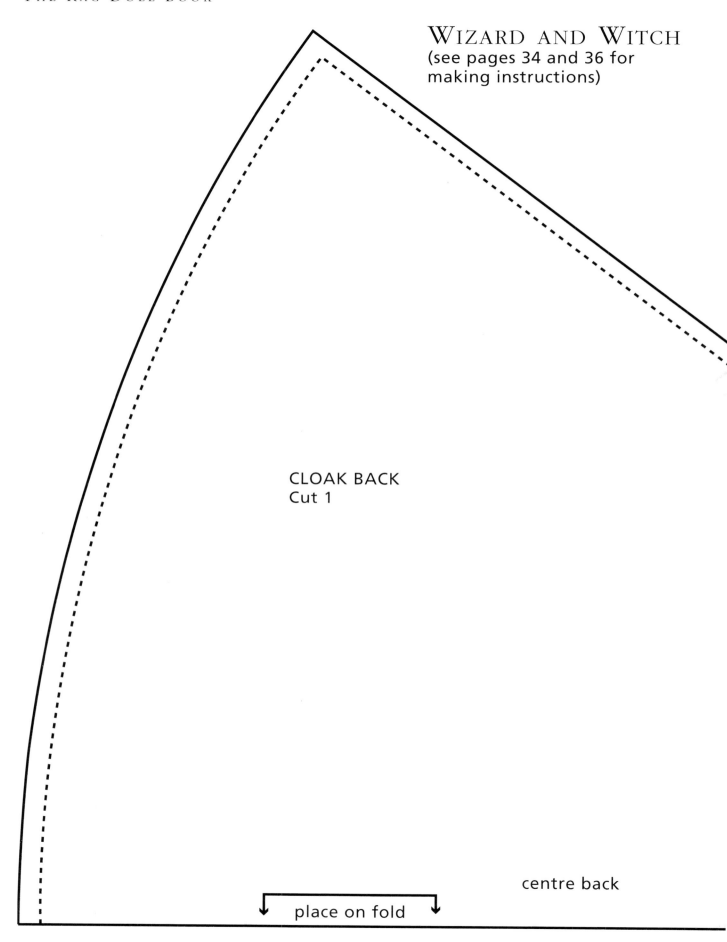

WIZARD AND WITCH
(see pages 34 and 36 for
making instructions)

CLOAK BACK
Cut 1

centre back

place on fold

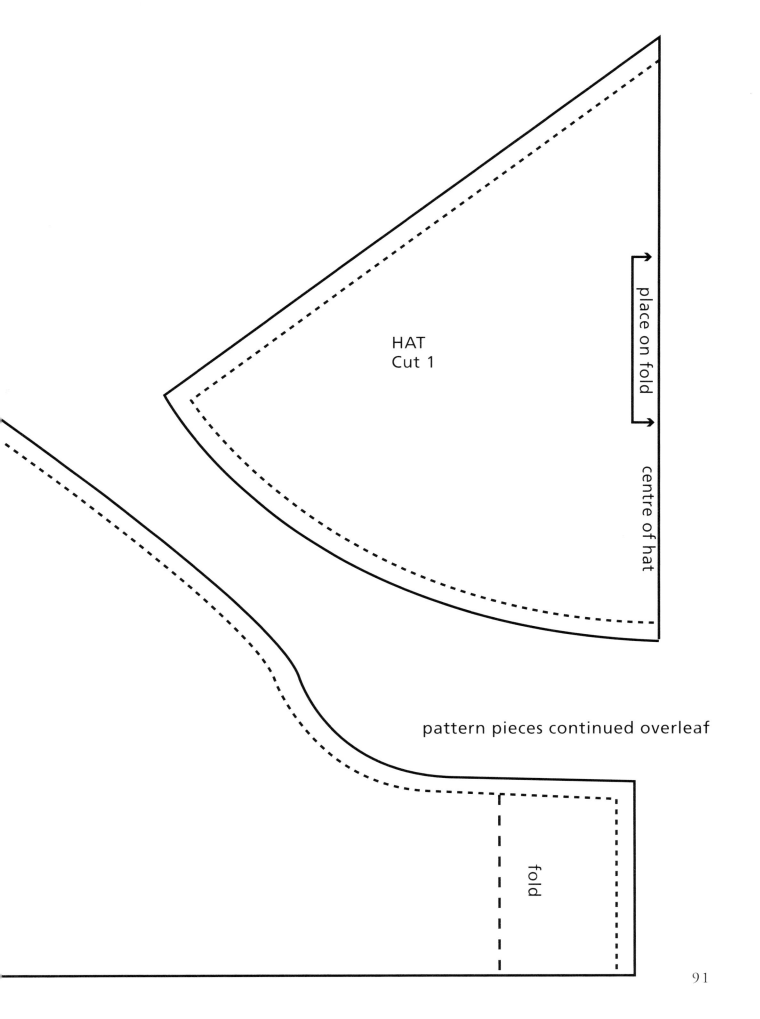

HAT
Cut 1

place on fold

centre of hat

fold

pattern pieces continued overleaf

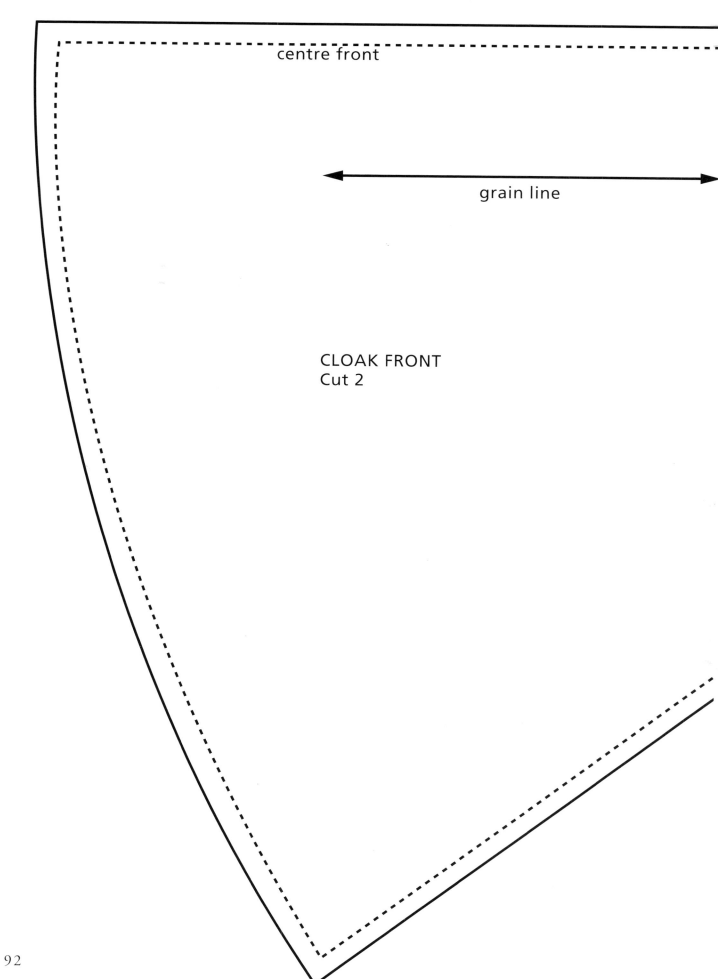

centre front

grain line

CLOAK FRONT
Cut 2

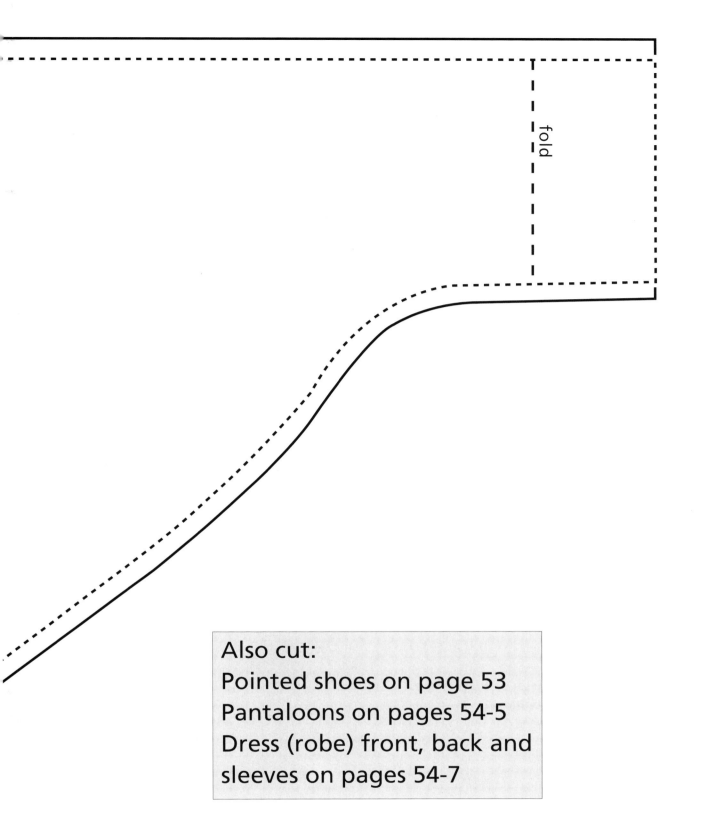

fold

Also cut:
Pointed shoes on page 53
Pantaloons on pages 54-5
Dress (robe) front, back and
sleeves on pages 54-7

Sailor Boy

(see page 38 for making instructions)

gather

place on fold

COLLAR
Cut 1

Also cut:
Thin doll's shoes on page 53
Trousers on pages 58-9
Shirt front, back and sleeves
on pages 60-1

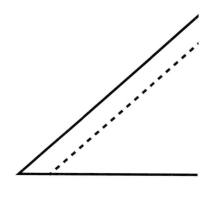

FATHER CHRISTMAS (see page 42 for making instructions)

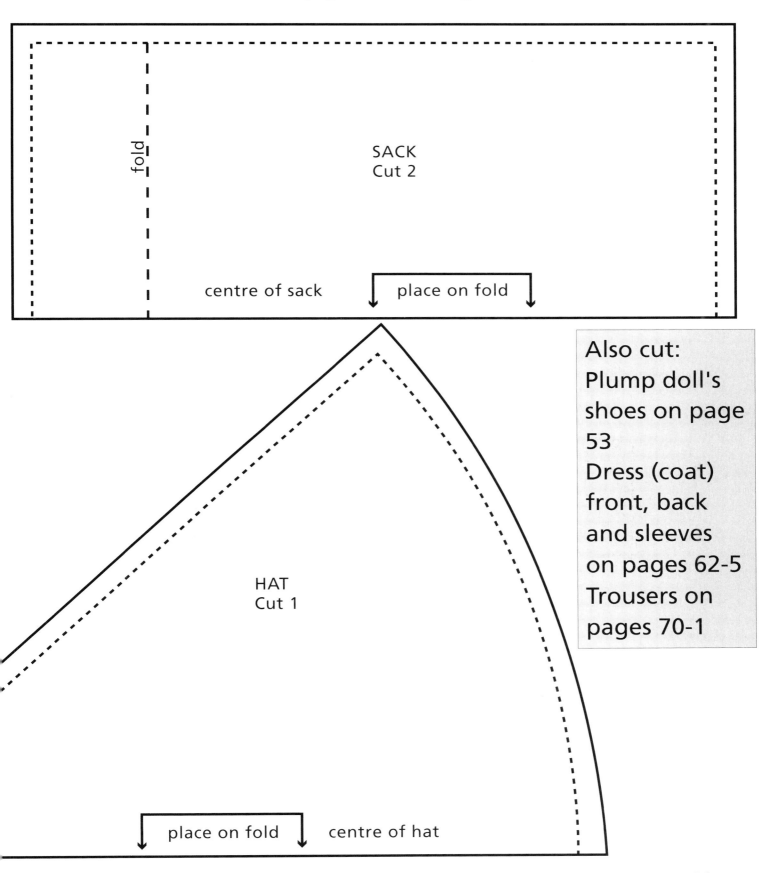

SACK
Cut 2

fold

centre of sack   place on fold

HAT
Cut 1

Also cut:
Plump doll's
shoes on page
53
Dress (coat)
front, back
and sleeves
on pages 62-5
Trousers on
pages 70-1

place on fold   centre of hat

STOCKISTS AND SUPPLIERS

In addition to your local haberdashers and second hand shops and car boot sales, there are some companies who supply all sorts of bits and pieces to accessorize your dolls' clothes.

FEATHERS, FELTS, BEADS, GLUES AND RAFFIAS

Fred Aldous Ltd
37 Lever Street
Manchester 1
M60 1UX
Telephone: 0161 236 2477

BEADS

Creative Beadcraft
Denmark Works
Sheepcote Dell Road
Beamond End
Nr Amersham
Bucks HP7 0RX
Telephone: 01494 715606

CM Offray & Son Ltd
Fir Tree Place
Church Road
Ashford
Middx TW15 2PH
Telephone: 01784 247281

RIBBONS

Ribbon Designs
42 Lake View
Edgware
Middx HA8 7RU
Telephone: 0181 958 4966

FABRIC DYES

Dylon International Ltd
London SE26 5HE
Telephone: 0181 663 4801

FABRIC PAINTS AND PENS

Atlascraft Ltd
Ludlow Hill Road
West Bridgford
Nottingham NG2 6HD
Telephone: 01602 452202

Decart
PO Box 309
Morrisville
VT 05661 USA
Telephone: (802) 888 4217

Jones Tones
68-743 Perez Road
D-16 Cathedral City
CA 92234 USA
Telephone: (800) 397 9667

Philip and Tacey Ltd
North Way
Andover
Hampshire SP10 5BA
Telephone: 01264 332171

Inscribe Ltd
The Woolmer Industrial Estate
Bordon
Hampshire GU35 9QE
Telephone: 01420 475747

Tulip
24 Prime Park Way
Natick
MA 01760 USA
Telephone: (508) 650 5400

ACKNOWLEDGMENTS

A big thank you to Cindy Richards at Ebury Press for asking me to work on this exciting project. To Emma Callery for editing the book and to friends, family and Jim for all their support. Also, thank you to Anne Boyes and Minna Simms for all their help.